HOW TO BE
A BRIDESMAID

ANG

WARD LOCK

Also by Angela Lansbury and published by Ward Lock:

How to Be the Best Man

The Wedding Planner

Wedding Etiquette

Wedding Speeches and Toasts

First published 1991 by Ward Lock
Villiers House, 41/47 Strand, London WC2N 5JE, England

A Cassell Imprint

British Library Cataloguing in Publication Data

Lansbury, Angela
    Family matters: how to be a bridesmaid
    1. Weddings. Planning
    I. Title
    395.22

    ISBN 0-7063-7003-1

Typeset in 11 on 11½ point ITC Garamond Light by
Columns Design and Production Services Ltd, Reading

Printed and bound in Great Britain by
William Collins & Sons, Glasgow

CONTENTS

ACKNOWLEDGEMENTS

For information, advice and quotations thanks to Berkertex; Pronuptia; Just Jane Bride & Maid; The Scottish Tartan Society in Scotland; Sonia King Turpin of the Federation of Image Consultants; Colour Consultant, Champneys; RNIB; RNID; Royal Association in Aid of Deaf People; The Tea Council; Saville Edells, personalised cushion suppliers of London and Los Angeles; Thomson Worldwide Weddings; Robbi Ernst III, Wedding Consultant, San Francisco, USA; Fisher Films, producers of wedding videos in Sydney, Australia.

INTRODUCTION

Fairy stories end with the princess marrying the prince but realistic little girls dream of being a bridesmaid, an ambition they can achieve at a younger age. One child even wrote to a London newspaper saying she had never been a bridesmaid and asking if any engaged couple needed one! Her wish was fulfilled. But you do not have to be a young girl to be a bridesmaid, or to enjoy being a central part of the joyous occasion of a wedding. It is a privilege to be a bridesmaid, and the experience is usually a great pleasure as you share in the trials, tribulations and triumph of the wedding of a close friend or relative.

Being a bridesmaid involves a lot of work but it can be great fun. Your good relationship with the bride should be improved and made closer by your enthusiasm, and you can offer great support at a time of considerable stress.

Your happy memories will include the shared time shopping for the clothes. You will laugh together over those little mishaps you were able to sort out just in time. Above all you will have those wonderful photographs, perhaps even a video of that special day, showing the bride and the bridesmaids looking their happiest and loveliest.

'A happy bridesmaid makes a happy bride,' wrote Alfred Lord Tennyson in *The Bridesmaid*, implying that a happy bridesmaid makes the bride happy and that eventually she herself will become a happy bride.

Tennyson also said, 'so much to do!' The role of the bridesmaid includes wearing clothes appropriate to the bride's dream wedding (and remember not all brides want bridesmaids rivalling them for attention) as well as supporting and soothing the bride so that both have happy memories.

The saying 'always a bridesmaid never a bride' or 'three times a bridesmaid never a bride' is not true. Lady Diana Spencer (the Princess of Wales) was bridesmaid to her sister Jane. You can be a bridesmaid many times. Princess Anne was a bridesmaid six times. My neighbour was a bridesmaid eight times and after marrying was matron of honour. Admittedly women who have never been bridesmaids marry, occasionally more than once. As a wit said of a much-married woman, 'Always a bride, never a bridesmaid'.

BEING CHOSEN

You don't invite yourself, saying, 'Can I be your bridesmaid?' The bride chooses her bridesmaids.

WHO CAN BE CHOSEN

The religion of the bridesmaid may be different from that of the bride and groom, especially if the bride and groom are of different faiths, and are perhaps considering a register office wedding. At an orthodox wedding check that the authorities accept the bridesmaid for the ceremony and that she knows whether she must pray and sing in public. Non-Jews cannot be attendants at orthodox Jewish weddings but they can be attendants at Conservative (USA) or Reform (UK) weddings.

WHO SHOULD BE CHOSEN

It is diplomatic to choose bridesmaids from both families, just as the groom will include the bride's brother or brothers amongst his ushers.

Family take precedence over friends. Usually the bride's oldest sister is her chief bridesmaid and young sisters the other bridesmaids. After that come cousins or nieces, especially if they live nearby, the bride knows them well and sees them often. If the bride has no sisters the groom's sister can be chief bridesmaid and his other sisters, nieces or cousins or her cousins and nieces will be the other bridesmaids. Finally, friends are chosen. If no family or friends are available the bride may choose children she knows well through her employment, especially if she is a teacher or nanny. Tiny tots who adore the bride and are seen regularly, even daily in the months leading up to the wedding, can still be given an important role even though members of her own family are available and already selected as bridesmaids.

If the bride wants a bridesmaid to help her organise the wedding – as would an older bride less dependent on her own mother, she may choose someone living nearby.

COST CONSTRAINTS

Since the bride or her family traditionally pays bridesmaids' expenses, she may limit the number of bridesmaids or have none if she has insufficient budget for finding their accommodation, paying for clothes and choosing a gift for each one (although the groom usually covers the latter).

PREGNANT ATTENDANTS

A pregnant attendant is perfectly acceptable. If she is married, as a matron of honour she can dress differently to the bridesmaids. If the wedding is a long distance away, remember that airlines will not accept passengers in advanced stages of pregnancy. Stress and air pressure might cause miscarriage or premature birth in mid-air risking diverting the plane to hospital. You wouldn't reach the wedding anyway!

PREGNANT BRIDESMAIDS

Pregnancy does not automatically disbar a bridesmaid. Find out if the vicar is likely to object to an unmarried mother being a bridesmaid. If he accepts a pregnant bride because he prefers her to get married he may concede that an engaged girl planning marriage should be encouraged to attend church.

A bridesmaid as part of a team has to dress like others who may have already chosen clothes. But the sole bridesmaid can order a concealing dress in a size larger to allow room for growth. A V-shaped dropped waistline helps, as does carrying a large bouquet. If no problems arise it is not kind to withdraw the invitation from a bridesmaid who becomes pregnant because this would disappoint her and make her feel unwanted at the wedding.

However, the pregnant bridesmaid might decline to avoid the combined stress of a difficult pregnancy plus a busy role as chief bridesmaid. During the engagement there are tiring trips to shops negotiating steps when she might have morning sickness and swollen ankles.

SECOND MARRIAGE

Any children of the bride and groom from previous marriages, whether the parent is single, divorced or widowed, have to be allotted roles so they do not feel neglected. Consult their feelings and perhaps let them choose their own roles. Children too young and shy to be adult bridesmaids can look after coats or fill champagne glasses.

WHEN YOU ARE CHOSEN

You can expect to receive a phone call or a letter with details of the time and place, who will be paying for the bridesmaids' dresses, where you can stay, and so on.

ACCEPTING GRACEFULLY

The tone of your letter depends on how well you know the bride. If she's your best friend she will probably have told you in person or phoned unless you live so far away that she has had to contact you by letter. In that case you just write expressing how happy you feel and follow up by phone as soon as you can.

REFUSING

If expected to pay for your own clothes and unable to meet this cost, you can decline graciously, especially if this would be the third wedding that year and the novelty of being a bridesmaid has worn off.

HANDICAPS AND ILLNESS

There is no reason why wheelchair-bound people should not be able to be bridesmaids. Sisters and friends with permanent disabilities can be included in the ceremony as bridesmaids or other attendants. A mentally handicapped adult who is not eligible as legal witness can still be a bridesmaid.
(See handicapped weddings, blind, deaf and wheelchair users, pages 74–77.)

REFUSAL LETTER AFTER ILLNESS/ACCIDENT/ OPERATION

Dear (bride's first name)
Thank you so much for inviting me to be your bridesmaid. It has made me (and whoever) very very happy to hear your good news. Unfortunately I am still weak after the foot operation and cannot be sure how soon I shall be able to travel and resume normal activities. Rather than disappoint everyone later I shall decline from the outset and plan to attend as your guest. My thoughts are with you. It must be such fun. I'll phone you soon to check that all is going well for the big day. All my/our love

Other reasons for refusing are exams, pregnancy, death in the family or contagious sickness or long illness, and inability to travel with children or leave children behind.

CANCELLED WEDDING

Listen sympathetically until a week has passed and the tiff or cancellation seems permanent. Then unflappably locate lists of gift donors and offer to help write brief notes accompanying returned gifts. Produce the newspaper phone number so the bride can announce the cancellation. The bride-not-to-be returns the engagement ring, engagement presents, shower gifts (see American weddings), wedding presents and is expected to refund the bridesmaids for any deposit on dresses.

Keep in touch to cheer up your friend. 'These things happen. Anyone can make a mistake. It's probably all for the best. There's someone for everyone.'

You cannot expect to be chosen as bridesmaid at the next wedding. The bride might have a smaller wedding and need to choose the groom's sister. She could hold the wedding far away where her new man cannot encounter people discussing her cancelled engagement. If you are chosen again repeating previous plans seems easier, but she may want to start afresh.

BRIDESMAIDS' AND ATTENDANTS' ROLES

This guide explains why you have been selected and other attendants have been allotted their roles. It may help you as chief bridesmaid to assist the bride in organising younger helpers.

In olden times the best man, while acting as bodyguard for the bride, might have been tempted to take her for himself, so later she was surrounded by bridesmaids while the best man stayed beside the groom.

The bride can have as many as twelve bridesmaids. The bride needs enough bridesmaids to carry the train, but preferably not too many. Other considerations are the formality and size of the wedding, not outnumbering the guests, and how many relatives must be honoured.

A bride without sisters can still have several bridesmaids, as did Princess Mary, in 1922. Her eight bridesmaids included Elizabeth, later the Queen Mother.

A bride who has no sisters may decide to choose cousins as bridesmaids. When Princess Anne married in 1973 she was attended by her younger brother, nine-year-old Prince Edward, and by her nine-year-old young cousin, Lady Sarah Armstrong-Jones, Princess Margaret's daughter. Anne, having been a bridesmaid herself six times, decided against having 'yards of uncontrollable children', as she explained on television.

When Princess Alexandra got married in 1963 she had five bridesmaids and two pageboys who wore kilts and black shoes with silver buckles. Afterwards the bridesmaids were given gold bracelets. The groom traditionally pays for such gifts to bridesmaids, which are very common.

Home videos you may have seen show that tiny bridesmaids look cute but can cause havoc. A group of three tiny tots should really sit during the ceremony as standing would tire them and they might cause a distraction. But a mature nine-year-old junior bridesmaid will probably be more composed and perfectly capable of standing demurely behind the bride.

A recent survey showed that the most popular number at the start of the 1990 decade was three bridesmaids and a pageboy.

DIFFERENT ATTENDANTS' ROLES

CHIEF BRIDESMAID

When there are two or more bridesmaids with a big age gap the older one is the chief bridesmaid. If two friends of similar ages are chosen the one who knows the bride better, or who lives nearer and therefore has a bigger helping role, is accorded this honour. Americans tend to favour having joint chief bridesmaids who walk together at the ceremony.

MAID OF HONOUR

As the bride is 'queen for the day' it is fitting that she should be attended by maids of honour. A sole bridesmaid cannot be chief bridesmaid. She is maid of honour. The bride can choose to have two maids of honour. For example, the bride's sister can take turns with the groom's sister so that they share the role. Alternatively the bride might pair a friend as maid of honour with her existing sister-in-law. Or if her brother is single and he has a live-in girlfriend she could be called maid of honour or the less specific American term honour attendant.

Maids of honour pastries are named after the maids of honour attending the queen or princess at the royal court. The maids supposedly baked custard tarts in puff pastry for the queen and themselves at a palace hen party and later for the queen and her guests.

MATRON OF HONOUR

A divorcee, widow or older bride is likely to choose a married friend to be an attendant. You can have two matrons of honour if the bride's older sister and best friend are both married. A matron is a married woman, perhaps the bride's older sister. An older helper such as the bride's mother or a substitute for the bride's mother (such as a married aunt) may take on the role. She acts as a secretary, companion and expert on everything! Certainly if she is older or has been married a long time she can offer the benefit of her experience of married life as well as her own wedding. It is considered lucky to have a matron of honour.

BRIDESMAIDS AS WITNESSES

Bridesmaids and groomsmen can all sign the register. If you plan to do this tell the vicar or priest in advance so that they can add extra lines so it looks neat. Of course you shouldn't sign unless you have been invited to do so. A junior/child bridesmaid can have the thrill of signing after two legal witnesses have signed. While we are discussing signatures – although not in this case as witnesses – a guest book or autograph book can be supplied for guests to sign on arrival at the reception, with the chief bridesmaid in charge of it. (See chapter on reception.)

As only two witnesses are required often the chief bridesmaid is the only one of several bridesmaids to carry out this role, the other witness being the best man.

WITNESS WITHOUT BRIDESMAIDS

When circumstances prevent bridesmaids being appointed, a favoured female friend of the bride might be chosen as witness.

The witness does not join in the church procession and recession nor wear distinctive clothes. The role of witness might be offered to a friend at a register office wedding.

APPOINTING A WITNESS IN ADDITION TO BRIDESMAIDS

This is a good solution for the bride who wishes to satisfy a sister who is unsuitable or unwilling to be a bridesmaid, or older sister-in-law with an important role. The advantage to the witness is that this means less cost and less fuss than being a bridesmaid. Perhaps an important female friend from abroad unexpectedly becomes able to attend the wedding and surprises the bride after bridesmaids and their dresses have been chosen; she too could be a witness.

ACTING WITNESS INSTEAD OF BRIDESMAID

The girl who declines to be a bridesmaid despite the bride's protest might please the bride by volunteering to be witness, although the reluctant bridesmaid should not insist on this role if another person has already been selected.

MOVING THE DIFFICULT BRIDESMAID

Sometimes one bridesmaid cannot agree on the dress style, shoe colour, or anything that the bride and other bridesmaids are happy with. Maybe she dislikes the other bridesmaid and is annoyed at having a rival, can't make up her mind about dress style, knows exactly what suits her and won't accept anything else, or can't afford the clothes but is too embarrassed to say so. The bride, who must decide when there is no agreement, can speed progress and please other bridesmaids by transferring the girl to the role of witness, and with luck, everyone will be happy.

WITNESS AT RENEWAL OF VOWS

At a second marriage or renewal of vows, when bridesmaids are not appropriate, female attendants can be honoured as witnesses. A couple in their forties renewed their vows 24 years after their first small wedding, this time as a grand occasion setting out stylishly in two stretch limousines with their four adult children as witnesses.

JUNIOR BRIDESMAID

The junior bridesmaid is a term applied to describe a bridesmaid age 8–14. The bride might have two or a group but there has to be a limit in numbers. More than twelve bridesmaids looks absurd but a class of school-girls could form a guard of honour at the church exit instead, pairs of girls holding clean hockey sticks or long-stemmed flowers to form an archway.

Bridesmaids aged under 8 can be either train-bearers or flower girls. The smallest girl has the least responsibility and merely carries a posy.

RING-BEARER

The ring-bearer is often a small boy carrying the ring, which is tied or loosely sewn onto a cushion with two ribbons. Tiny children who cannot be entrusted with a gold ring carry a sumbolic substitute which is not used during the ceremony. The ring-bearer walks ahead of the bride in the procession but need not stand during the ceremony. Being ring-bearer gives him a job which makes him feel important – and keeps his hands respectably occupied. The ring-bearer could be a little girl – the choice depends on the numbers of children of each sex who are allotted roles.

FLOWER GIRL OR BOY

The flower girl or boy carries flower petals, whole flowers or confetti. She gives flowers to guests on either side of the aisle before or during the procession.

The flower girl dresses differently from bridesmaids. She might be the daughter of the bride's sister or best friend. If the bride chooses a small niece she needs to have an older bridesmaid who can take charge of the young child.

In the recession the flower girl walks before the bride, unlike bridesmaids, in order to scatter flower petals at the church door as the bride exits, throwing more while walking ahead of the bride along the churchyard path. Check in advance how far she should progress and that the church does not object. There may be a ban on petals inside the church on carpets in case people slip on them, a stipulation about the type of material that can be thrown, or a charge for sweeping up.

PRESENTER OF LUCKY HORSESHOE

A lucky horseshoe can be handed to the bride in her recession down the church aisle or on the steps of the church afterwards. The bride may be given several lucky horseshoes, by her mother, the chief bridesmaid, a small niece, and other well-wishers. Write a goodwill message on the back of the gift and sign it so she knows who her lucky horseshoes are from. The lucky horseshoe is silvery, or padded white satin, lace-edged and held over the bride's arm by a silk ribbon. Small rolling pins, Welsh love spoons and other favours produced commercially are sold in bridal shops. They are also sold by specialized cookware shops for decorating wedding cakes. Or make your own cardboard lucky black cat or chimney sweep picture for a child to present.

BABY BRIDESMAID

The baby bridesmaid can be a general nuisance, crawling up the aisle, cooing at guests, or peeping under the bride's dress. Usually the bride's daughter, sister, or niece has to be carried by her mother, father, granny, or nanny even if she is nominally a bridesmaid. During the marriage ceremony and church service babies should be kept at the back so that if they cry or need changing they can be taken out quickly and unobtrusively. The church or cathedral may ban pushchairs or allow them only partway into the building, not near the steps leading to the altar.

As the baby cannot walk she/he does not do much except be photographed sitting on the bride's lap (perhaps on a cushion over a piece of waterproof cloth to prevent unpleasant accidents!) or beside the bride in the carriage.

Somebody must be in charge of changing the baby, not the bride in her white dress, nor bridesmaids wearing their expensive gowns. Spare nappies and a second baby's dress are advisable.

Babies are likely to fall asleep. I saw a prettily decorated white pushchair with white sunshade at a wedding reception that showed thoughtfulness and practicality. A rocking cradle on wheels with white canopy can be brought along, assuming the bride agrees, providing you can get the cradle up steps into the building. This saves going home early to babysit or deliver to a babysitter.

BEST GIRL

Just as the bride can have a male pageboy as well as bridesmaids, the groom can choose a female attendant. The best girl is the closest female relative (such as his twin sister, sister, mother or aunt) or closest friend (such as the flatmate or business partner). It is still rather unusual.

Checklist – Names and roles

Attendants' Names:

Best Man ....

Chief usher ....

Ushers/Groomsmen ....

Matron of Honour ....

Chief Bridesmaid or Maid of Honour ....

Adult Bridesmaids ....

Junior Bridesmaids ....

Pageboy(s) ....

Flower Girl ....

Presenter of horseshoe to bride ....

Presenter of bouquet to bride's mother ....

Reader(s) during service:

    minister ....../ second minister ....../bridesmaid(s) ....../

    other ....

Singers during service: church choir/
bridesmaid(s)/other ....

Guard of Honour ....

Witnesses ....

Roles for: Bride's Sisters ....; Bride's brothers ....;
groom's brothers ...., groom's sisters ....,
groom's cousins ...., bride's cousins ....,
groom's nieces and nephews ...., bride's nieces
and nephews ...., bride's adult friends ....,
bride's pupils ...., bride's married relatives and
friends ...., matron of honour's child; best man's
child ....; step-sisters ....; step-children ....

Roles: carrying train, carrying bouquet, carrying bride's
ring, carrying bride's prayerbook, witnesses, flower
girls, holding hen party, entertaining visiting guests,
hosting and serving at reception.

Total number of attendants ...... Are they paired? Yes/No

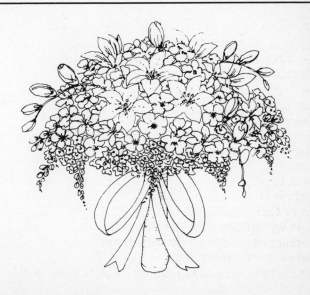

CLOTHES

ROYAL WEDDING STYLES

Queen Victoria married in a dress of white satin and Honiton lace and a wreath of orange blossom in 1840. This century we have had some wonderful royal weddings video-recorded so you can replay every gorgeous minute and decide if there are any features of their ceremonies and dresses you would like to copy. The royal wedding dresses alongside those of the attendants are periodically on display.

Princess Diana married in an ivory silk taffeta and lace dress, hand embroidered with pearls and mother of pearl sequins. It had a low neckline, puff sleeves, and a full skirt supported by a stiff petticoat. The 25 foot train was edged with lace.

The five bridesmaids wore ivory silk taffeta dresses, the same material as Diana's dress, with double skirts co-ordinating with the bride's dress, puff sleeves like the bride's decorated with ribbon bows, and golden silk sashes. The dresses were different lengths, full length for the oldest girl, calf length for intermediate age. The flowers they carried echoed flowers in their hair.

Diana's pageboys wore the dress uniform of naval cadets of 1863, dark jackets, light trousers, helmets, white gloves, and swords to echo the uniform of Prince Charles, who wore the full dress uniform of a Commander of the Royal Navy.

Within hours of Princess Anne's wedding, copies of

the wedding dress appeared in chain stores bearing the promise 'Feel like a princess'. Princess Anne's dress was princess line with no seam at the waist and a flared skirt. Her epaulettes echoed those on the military attire of her groom, the bodice had pintucks and long two layer sleeves with chiffon.

Princess Anne's bridesmaid Lady Sarah wore an ankle-length dress which looked like a long-sleeved dress, actually a white pinafore dress over a blouse with ruffled collar, and a Juliet cap or skull cap. Princess Anne's younger brother Edward wore highland dress. Princess Anne's pageboy wore a kilt and sporran, dark jacket and white jabot (frill), black shoes and tartan socks.

When Sarah Ferguson married Prince Edward her four bridesmaids wore peach dresses. The two younger pageboys wore white sailor suits, while the two other boys dressed differently. You can see many pictures of this and other royal weddings in books about the royal family.

WHO PAYS?

Traditionally the head of the household in the bride's family pays for bridesmaids' dresses. In the days when girls married from home at 16 and unmarried daughters had no income the bride's father paid. Nowadays an older bride living apart from her parents with her own income often pays for some of the wedding and the bridesmaid's dress herself. When the bride has left home to live with a man their wedding celebrations are sometimes funded from their own household budget.

The parents or mother of young bridesmaids and small attendants generally pay for their clothes, unless the bride's family are much more affluent and insist on meeting the cost.

The best girl is the groom's assistant so theoretically he pays for accessories he stipulates, and her corsage. But the best girl is not involved in undue expense. She is not required to dress like the bridesmaids and can wear whatever clothing she likes, providing it is equally formal and not clashing with other people's colours.

COST OF CLOTHES

An off-the-peg bridesmaid's dress can be quite expensive. If the bride's family is paying for the clothes she may be unable to afford to have many bridesmaids, or she may budget carefully when choosing the dresses. Bridesmaids must not look disappointed and insist on having the most expensive dress in the shop. Dresses for adult bridesmaids can be hired, as can hats and party dresses, and this is often an excellent idea.

When shopping together for styles and prices don't point to clothes beyond the bride's price range and say 'I like this' or ask 'Why don't you have that?'. Be frank with shop assistants who ask your budget. Phone in advance of your visit and ask how wide their range is and the average cost.

A bridesmaid who wants, say, exceptionally expensive shoes might offer to buy her own shoes. If a small bridesmaid is growing so fast that she always needs new shoes her mother might be happy to pay for white or coloured shoes.

BRIDE'S CLOTHES' STYLE

Bridesmaids can accompany the bride and probably her mother to help her select the bridal gown. Two excursions may be made, first the fact-finding tour, then the decision-making trip. The bride's dress must be selected first so that the bridesmaids' dresses co-ordinate with its style. The main shops can be found by looking through the telephone directory, local news-papers and bridal magazines, driving around nearby high streets, asking brides, visiting bridal shows, and phoning department stores.

At some shops the bride can have a dress designed for her by the in-house designer, but the cost can run into thousands of pounds or dollars. Elaborate dresses have overskirts bo-peep style with the top layer of material raised in scallops caught up with bows. Satin is cheaper than silk.

Hiring can be about half the price, and some suppliers suggest bridesmaids should shop and order better dresses about a year in advance. You may need another size dress or four girls' dresses when only one is in stock. The dress itself can be made in another colour, or with ribbon rose decorations in a different colour. It usually takes 8–12 weeks for delivery from manufacturer to shop. Try on dresses about one or two months before the wedding and allow time for alterations.

ENGLISH, SCOTTISH AND IRISH

White tie is very formal and used in mainland Britain for occasions attended by royalty or the prime minister but it is also popular for weddings in Ireland. The bride should discuss the men's clothing with the groom. If tail coats are required traditional long dresses for the bride and bridesmaids look well. The men may feel that tail coats are an old-fashioned nuisance, like the young men in Tuxedo who cut the tails off their coats so that Americans since then have called a dinner jacket a Tuxedo. Modern vivid colours will go well with black dinner jackets, or pastel colours with white dinner jackets.

Scottish grooms and best men can wear tartan kilts at the ceremony. Bridesmaids rarely do but dressmakers can make bridesmaids' dresses in tartan.

Scottish bridesmaids might wear a sash diagonally over one shoulder in their clan tartan at a dance. Tartan sashes are worn up over the right shoulder and fastened on the shoulder by a small pin or brooch, except for chieftainesses and wives of colonels of Scottish regiments who wear the sash over the left shoulder. The sash ends hang down from the shoulder to below the waist, one end forward, one back. When dancing both ends can hang backwards, the underneath piece fastened at the back at waist level by a belt or buttons.

After marriage the bride or matron of honour can still wear her original tartan but she has a longer sash worn upside down so that it can be tied in a bow on her left hip. Family, military and corporate tartans can be worn to give a unified look.

JEWISH, ARAB AND JAPANESE

Jewish brides like to be covered up to the neck as modest dress is expected in a synagogue.

Arab brides also like high necks, long-sleeved, ankle-length dresses which are heavily beaded. Arabs might order up to four dresses, one in white ivory, another pink, for a four-day wedding. An Arab bridesmaid likewise might have two to four outfits.

Japanese brides like off-the-shoulder dresses. The Japanese have two dresses, perhaps a white gown for the ceremony, a pink dress for the reception, then a kimono as well.

ATTENDANTS' DRESS STYLES

BRIDESMAIDS' DRESS STYLES

Styles must co-ordinate with the bride's dress but also suit the ages of the bridesmaids. Long ago children were dressed like miniature adults, but nowadays the tendency is to have different styles for different ages. For example a fifteen-year-old prefers and looks more appropriate in a reasonably sophisticated dress, not too much like a little girl's frock.

MATRON OF HONOUR'S CLOTHES

The matron of honour's clothes are different from those worn by younger unmarried girls, and may have to look suitable for going to a registrar's office. A matron of honour staying at the bride's house the night before needs a neat outfit for travelling there, with clothes packed in a smart overnight bag or suitcase.

A matron of honour's dress can be bought from the mother-of-the-bride section in bridal wear shops. Needless to say, a lively slim young woman in her twenties doesn't want to dress like a staid stout woman of fifty. An older matron of honour must be distinguishable from the bride's mother if they are similar ages.

The matron of honour may wear something removable to provide the bride with 'something borrowed', such as blue garter or blue brooch. The borrowed item symbolises friendship, and remains a popular tradition at many weddings.

YOUNGER BRIDESMAIDS

It is well worthwhile choosing an outfit for younger bridesmaids which is suitable for wear afterwards.

FLOWER GIRL

The flower girl can match or dress differently to other bridesmaids as is appropriate, although she oftens wears white. She carries a small posy or a basket of paper rose petals, basket and flower colours co-ordinating. Flower girls and pages, if paired, could dress in white sillk or satin.

PAGEBOY

Pageboy outfits are found in men's outfitters and bridal wear shops. Traditional pageboy outfits have tight pantaloon trousers fastened below the calf with buttons or ribbons. A red velvet suit with a red velvet tie can be hired.

Small boys often wear white, blue or grey miniature lounge suits, sometimes three piece, *i.e.* with a waistcoat. A junior kilt outfit with black velvet jacket looks good if the family is Scottish and the groom also wears a kilt. The jabot, the frill on the shirtfront, and the sporran, the fur-covered pouch hung in front of the kilt, are hired with the outfit. Accessories may be included or could cost extra.

To match a bridesmaid in white and blue a pageboy could wear a blue and white sailor suit. Little Lord Fauntleroy and Kate Greenaway suits with high waist trousers fit romantic period fashions. Tiny boys are sometimes paired in co-ordinating colours with junior bridesmaids in orange, brown or peach colour satin trousers and peach colour shirts with frills. Baby pink for toddlers, which is rather girlish, can be edged with blue piping.

You can see the different styles such as the Eton suit by writing to hire companies for their leaflets or looking in illustrated dictionaries and encyclopaedias. If you are having bridesmaids dresses made velvet pageboy outfits can be designed with lace collars to co-ordinate with the bridesmaids' and bride's dress.

RING-BEARER

The ring-bearer always dresses in white, goes the tradition, but others say he can be dressed in blue. In summer the ringbearer can be all white, wearing white suit, white shirt, white tie, white socks and white shoes. The ring could be pinned onto a white cushion.

BABY BRIDESMAID

The child's Christening gown can be worn or any frilly white party dress to co-ordinate with the bride if there are no other bridesmaids, or a coloured dress matching other bridesmaids.

COLOURS

Colour of Dresses
The aim is always to co-ordinate with bride's outfit. Any colour goes except all-white which can be confused with the bride and detracts from her uniqueness.

Don't be identical to the bride's colour or clash with it. A cream coloured bride's dress might co-ordinate better with a peach colour dress and flowers. Dresses could be in rainbow colours, or graduated shades of the same colour. Two blonde bridesmaids could wear pale blue, two brunettes darker blue or silver grey in the same style.

Bridesmaids in the 1990s wear peach, lilac, lemon, blue, or turquoise dresses. Pink, blue and gold are said to be lucky, and red and green unlucky. Green is considered unlucky in Ireland because it is the fairies' colour and the fairies might steal the wearer away. Superstition should not affect your rational judgement. Deeper colours, the modern fashion, look striking on dark-skinned brides and bridesmaids at sunny outdoor weddings surrounded by brightly coloured plants. Red and white is popular at Christmas time. Red and pure white looks harsh like 'blood and bandages', they say in army-base towns. Ivory white softens the contrast with red and other colours.

Check the church carpet colours and whether red carpet will be laid down, clashing with orange, pink or purple dresses. If so, you could ask the florist to supply white carpet.

BLACK DRESSES

Avoid complete black as it looks like mourning and is less jolly. A few people wish to reverse the trend and wear black at weddings to look sophisticated, and white at funerals to express confidence that the departed was a pure innocent soul who is now in heaven. Until the trend reverses completely this is likely to cause confusion. It also offends conservative grandparents who don't wish to be reminded of funerals and who like the bride in traditional white and bridesmaids in cheerful colours.

Patterned bridesmaids dresses are comparatively rare, though vertical pink and white striped cotton or pink and lavender mottled sheen satin dresses have been chosen. The joins of patterned fabric look neater when separated by piping in a plain colour such as pink along seams.

STYLE

Avoid inadvertently offending others or deliberately disregarding convention. Outfits which appear amusingly different in the shop can look very odd in church and halls full of elderly relatives. You might regret your decision too late on the day.

NECKLINES

Revealingly low necklines are unsuitable in church. If you want a strapless dress for dancing later, wear a bolero or jacket of matching material in church to cover your shoulders, upper arms, and suggestive cleavage. A removable collar can be added to a dress, and another option is to wear a shawl.

Enquire whether the minister objects to sleeveless, strapless dresses, for he might feel you were showing disrespect, making a mockery of him and his church.

In hot countries such as Australia, especially in summer, church authorities may be more easygoing. Unusual wedding outfits were accepted on one occasion by a minister in robes conducting a marriage in Sydney. The bride, wearing a tight white strapless dress, was followed by three bridesmaids in tight black strapless dresses. All the dresses had love heart plunge necklines. This wedding was filmed and replayed on Australian television. The effect was stunning because the bride was exceptionally glamorous.

Brides can marry in less conventional clothing such as flowing white trouser suits in UK register offices.

MAKING THE RIGHT IMPRESSION

Some brides go as far as hiring an image consultant to spend a day or two shopping with the bride and bridesmaids and advising them. On their shopping day the bride and bridesmaids and the consultant visit many stores and come home with notes to discuss what they like most. When the bride or chief bridesmaid particularly like a dress the shop will put it aside for a day or two while you dream about how you look in it.

The bridesmaids' dresses must not clash with the girls' uniform look. The bridesmaids' lipstick will be the same colour as the bride's but can be a darker or lighter shade to tone with their skin colouring. For example, a black bride having a register office wedding chose a white dress with navy trim and a matching hat with navy trim and navy shoes. To brighten the outfit the colour consultant suggested pink lipstick and flowers. The bridesmaids wore pink lipstick in different shades and navy dresses.

Discuss how the style of each dress suits each bridesmaid. The height of the girls affects the style but the length of different parts of her body determines which features should be disguised or enhanced. For example a short girl with long legs might be advised to wear a short jacket to the waist to emphasize her long legs, or not to wear a contrasting colour belt but a self-colour belt of the same material as the dress in order not to cut the body in half but accentuate the upward line. Small girls should avoid large patterns. A print with huge flowers will look odd if there's only room for one complete flower on your bosom. Also consider accessories. A small hat will not dwarf a smaller girl.

Generally a dark-skinned girl wears strong colours, dark colours or bright colours because these suit her skin tone but personality affects this too. A shy girl might prefer quieter colours. White comes in many shades. Ivory is a slightly yellow tinge. There are also grey whites, blue whites, pink whites, and green whites. Accessories can tone in, such as the navy accessories with a blue white.

When asked your opinion do not insult the bride by making her feel she has shortcomings. Avoid saying, 'that would look lovely on someone taller', implying she is too short. Don't upset the shop assistant by saying that a dress is terribly old-fashioned or the price is ridiculously expensive. You may be upsetting a customer who was considering buying it or another girl could emerge from the fitting room wearing it. If asked your opinion simply say to the bride, 'It's not you,' or 'It doesn't suit you'.

SEASONAL CLOTHES

A strapless gown supplied with a matching jacket is useful covering outdoors in cooler weather, or indoors in air conditioning and evening. Otherwise you may need a wrap. Clothing must be adaptable to the time of day. In hot countries it can be hot at noon and chilly at five o'clock after the sun sinks. Fans are handy in scorching weather in summer in Mediterranean countries, the Caribbean, much of the USA, Hong Kong, Japan or China. In the UK romantic fans fit period costumes.

Fabrics are heavier in winter. Bridesmaids could wear velvet dresses with fur trim and overjackets, warm muffs and fur-trimmed hats. For a register office attendants can wear coat-dresses.

THEMES

The reception surroundings and decor can inspire themes, such as Victorian, Edwardian, Art Deco or Roaring Twenties. Locations such as a lake, river or seaside suggest boating and sailor blue. Country gardens inspire green accessories and greenery in a hall or marquee with pillars decorated like trees to resemble a forest.

ALTERATIONS AND FITTING

An appointment is made for fitting dresses which have been made to order. A return visit is made about a week later to check that alterations are correct. When several bridesmaids have dresses of the same length it is well worth making an appointment to ensure that hem lengths are the same.

The alterations department may agree to adapt your dress afterwards so you can wear it again. In wartime dresses were made as blouses and skirts so that one half could be easily adapted for other occasions. The bridesmaid's dress could be altered by shortening the skirt and removing ribbons. Otherwise you could advertise the dresses for sale in local newspapers stating the sizes and colours, or take pictures and place advertisements in local shop windows.

Bridal shops supply dress covers in varying lengths. Clear covers are better for identifying bridesmaids' gowns. A white cover conceals the bride's secret dress. A bridal and ballgown clothing cover, flared to accommodate full skirts, can be bought through dry cleaning shops. It will protect long dresses in wardrobes and is useful for transporting clothes to the bride's house for dressing there on the wedding day or when travelling abroad.

MADE TO MEASURE MAIL ORDER

A London-based bridesmaid went to a wedding in the USA where all the bridesmaids had the same design dress made to measure in advance. She posted a list of her measurements for the dress to the USA. When she arrived in the USA and put the dress on it fitted perfectly. She had bought her own shoes in England which she had dyed to match the swatch of material she was sent.

DYEING ACCESSORIES

Obtain a fabric sample from the dress if you are dyeing shoes to match and send the sample to out-of-town bridesmaids. Plain or moiré silk shoes can be dyed to match dresses or sashes. Satin shoes should retain the sheen to match the dress or sash after dyeing, and cheaper shoes may turn out matt. Ask the dyers in advance if the shoes will retain their texture.

Shoes and clutch bags can be professionally dyed to match several outfits for the big trip to a wedding abroad. Use tea in a stainless steel bowl to dye all the bridesmaids' tights to match and turn shoes, stockings, gloves and lace from white to beige cream colour. Practise on old cloth first.

SHOES

The same shoes should be worn by all the bridesmaids for a uniform appearance. Court shoes and satin pumps are popular for wearing with bridal gowns and bridesmaids' dresses. Clip-on bows individualise the design. Ballet slippers with suede soles can be made up with your own fabric for child or adult bridesmaids (needing half a yard or more fabric per pair).

For weddings and formal occasions such as the rehearsal dinner, do not wear open toes nor backless or strapback shoes because they look too casual. Smart silver and gold strap sandals exposing feet look wrong with clothes that cover women up to the neck and down to the ankle. Edwardian bootees go with Edwardian dresses and bonnets from days when a lady did not expose her ankle, and top hats match Edwardian ladies' long-skirted riding habits.

Choose shoes that are easy to walk and dance in. Ankle straps help to anchor shoes, and you can also roughen the soles with sandpaper so that you do not slip. Wear in new shoes around the house in advance and ease tight leather shoes using a liquid product which stretches shoes while you wear them.

HEEL HEIGHT

A chief bridesmaid who is no taller than the next bridesmaid can wear higher heels to show who has precedence and neatly grade heights in the procession and photographs. One-inch heels with wider bases are better for walking than the spindly two-inch heels, or wobbling on glamorous but impractical three-inch heels.

CHILDREN'S SHOES

Black patent shoes can be worn by the pageboy. Little girls often wear white shoes and white party socks which can be bought from smart dress shops or bridal outfitters, socks made of finest cotton with trimming of lace and little white bows.

HOSIERY

White, ivory or flesh colour stockings and tights can be obtained, patterned with wedding bells, heart and ribbons, horseshoes, glitter hearts, usually on the back of the ankle. A line of pearls can be worn down the back or the outside of the leg. Avoid stockings with black seams.

UNDERCLOTHES

Lingerie will include pretty petticoats designed to be seen when you are dancing. A basque is worn under a strapless dress. Bra straps should be fastened to loops under dress shoulders. Underwear should not show through see-through materials and do not wear black underwear below pale colour dresses. Don't forget the garter!

Frilly underpants may be chosen for girls aged up to six and tomboys likely to do handstands.

ACCESSORIES

Sashes and other accessories might co-ordinate with the colours of the groomsmen's ties and cummerbunds and flower colours. Either give a dress material swatch to the groomsmen when they go to the hirers to get the right shade of blue or pink ties, or have cravats and accessories made up to match the dresses.

GLOVES

At formal weddings with short-sleeved dresses long gloves are worn, with long-sleeved dresses short gloves. An orthodox bride in a short-sleeved dress wears long gloves. From the 1920s until the 1950s a bridesmaid might have worn long gloves with buttons down the centre of the inner forearm. She wore the gloves when shaking hands but removed them from fingers for eating. They were not removed entirely but unbuttoned and the hand covering section was folded inside the forearm section. To match a dress with a net bodice wear net gloves.

JEWELLERY

Bridesmaids wear the minimum of jewellery to achieve a co-ordinated look. Accessories should not destroy the image or period the bride has created. Avoid incongruous colours or styles, no modern jewellery with old world clothes. Don't rival the bride, nor distinguish yourself from the group. Co-ordinate with the bride's jewellery whether gold, silver or two-colour jewellery combining gold and silver. Don't wear three pairs of ear-rings, heavy gold chains around ankles, or jingling bangles which are a distraction during the ceremony and speeches. The bride may be giving you jewellery. (See also Jewish weddings.)

To cover bitten nails you can buy false nails, which should not be obtrusively long. Nine carat gold nails (available at shops or through jewellery and mail order catalogues) are suitable only if the bride wears them.

WATCHES

Don't forget to turn off a watch alarm so it doesn't sound during the ceremony. With evening clothes wear a suitable dress watch *e.g.* goldplated with diamonds or diamonte stones set in the watchface. Smart black-face watches with small glinting stones can be found at reasonable cost.

Watches co-ordinating with bridesmaids' dresses are available in solid colours, for example an all pink watch

with pink face, pink edge and pink watchstrap can look wonderful. Watches can be bought with five interchangeably coloured bezels to match the bridesmaid dress and party clothes.

SPECTACLES

Ultra-modern frames are incongruous with period wedding gowns, so the bespectacled bridesmaid may prefer to remove her glasses for the procession. If glasses are needed for reading to sign your name, or driving, keep them in a padded glasses case in a wristbag.

Red glasses look wrong with pink dresses. For ultimate glamour the bride and her sisters can buy glasses in several colours matching dresses for entertaining.

PARASOLS

Pretty parasols, purely decorative in most English summers, are supplied in matching fabrics by bridal wear or accessory shops. When marrying abroad in hot countries parasols are practical for shielding you from sunburn, stickiness and exhaustion, helping you look cool and calm. The Caribbean is subject to sudden showers so a waterproof parasol is handy. Wet monsoon seasons strike South Pacific areas such as Hong Kong, Singapore and Australia.

HEAD-DRESS

Hats with matching handbags can be hired. Hats made to order using dress material or contrasting fabric can be kept or sold back to hat hire shops after one use.

Flower wreaths can be worn in the hair using reasonably priced fresh flowers in spring. Matching flower head-dress and posies can be made of silk flowers, a circlet of flowers for the smaller girls. Shapes include combs with attached flowers and mock pearls, arcs, diadems, glittering tiaras (popular with Indians), circular caps with hanging ribbons, ribbon roses and veils, and huge saucer shape hats.

FLOWERS

Flower colours contrast or co-ordinate with the dresses or overall colour theme *e.g.* red, white and blue; white, yellow and green; or shades of pink to purple in graduating colours.

The bride carries the most dramatic bouquet, the bridesmaids carrying similar but smaller or less elaborate flower arrangements. Bouquets should suit heights and builds of bridesmaids; cascades for tall girls, small flowers in the hair of dainty girls, and affordable flowers on wrists for economy. Pomanders attached to the wrists are convenient when holding the bride's train. It might be a good idea to attach the lightweight flowers a small bridesmaid carries to her wrists with bands of ribbon. Small children need styles which are almost indestructible!

The maid or matron of honour has different flowers from the bridesmaids. If you are slightly pregnant, confide in the bride and perhaps you will be able to hide the bump behind a big bouquet.

The groom pays for the flowers and his mother may accompany you to the flower shop. You have to agree on whether to have fresh or false flowers of silk or other fabric. The main considerations are the cost and availability of fresh flowers, (although fresh lilies can be flown in), whether you plan preserving the bouquet, and whether attendants have allergies.

Different bouquets are provided for honour attendants, corsages with street clothes, bouquets with short dresses. Long-stemmed sheaves are carried on the outside arm with flowerheads pointing outwards. Baskets and bouquets are carried in front. Heather is used with Scotland dress. Small girls can carry hoops entwined with ribbons and flowers.

ALLERGY

You don't want to sneeze throughout the ceremony. Hay fever and asthmatic attacks are inconvenient and embarrassing. The church or register office may be already decorated with flowers so you might have to endure them briefly. Sometimes at the church or synagogue the bride for a following wedding has paid for flowers to be installed, so you might get a nasty surprise! Small flower displays at the reception probably won't affect you providing you are not sitting next to them.

Avoid spending hours carrying a bouquet of fresh flowers. Dried flower bouquets are not necessarily the solution – one bouquet had to be left with a relative for six months until it stopped causing irritation. Fortunately fake flowers can be indistinguishable from real ones, and these are often the answer to this problem.

RING-BEARER CUSHIONS

Ring-bearer cushions are sold in the UK, USA and Australia. The cushion often has a lace frill around the edge, a strap underneath for the hands to hold it when not in use, and two ribbons which can be used to tie on the ring with a bow. The ring cushion can be heart-shape, circular, oval, oblong or square. A heart-shaped motif can be outlined in mock pearls in the centre. The chief bridesmaid may have to carry the cushion and give it to the child at the last moment, or supervize the child holding it. The ring might be tied on in advance, but practice making a neat bow. Alternatively the ring can be tied on in the church entry hall before proceeding. To practical people symbolic rings seem pointless, but are sometimes carried by toddlers to give them a role.

Checklist – Clothes

Bridal wear shops:

Name ....

Address .... phone ....

    opening hours .... late night opening ....

    nearest train/parking .... our assistant ....

    dress styles preferred .... cost ....

Shoe shops ....

Groom's clan kilt .... Toastmaster's clan kilt ....

Scottish thistle and heather buttonholes. Scottish heather in bride's bouquet. Welsh daffodils.

Bridal dress stocklist .... delivery to shop date ....
fitting date .... delivery to home date ....
Bride's dress fabric, bride's dress colour; bride's dress style;
Her shoes, head-dress, gloves, tights; bouquet, parasol, jewellery.
Something old .... Something new ....
Something borrowed .... Something blue ....
Chief bridesmaid's dress fabric, colour, style, ribbon colour, head-dress, gloves, shoes, tights, jewellery, flowers. Parasol/other accessories ....
Flower girl's dress colour, shoes, tights, flower basket.
Pageboy's outfit, shoes, and accessories (e.g. ring cushion).
Co-ordinating colours: groom and groomsmen's suits, their accessories ....
Mother of bride .... mother of groom ....
matron of honour; female witness;
church carpet .... reception carpet ....
car colours ....
For travelling and hanging bridesmaid dress covers.
(Bridal dresses should not be stored indefinitely in polythene or they may go yellow.)
Clothes supplier's names and address and phone ....
Delivery date and time ....
Guard of Honour's uniforms and flowers, school scarves, hockey sticks, tennis raquets, golf clubs, fencing swords, swords?
Is bride's father paying for clothes? ....
Insurance (your household policy, bride's wedding insurance policy)

OTHER PRE-WEDDING PLANS

If the bride is a laugh-a-minute, accident-prone type who you might have to help out of scrapes, get her organised. If you share a bedroom, rearrange it so she has everything to hand in a top drawer with a folder containing vital papers. Give her an address book with reference headings such as Caterers, Florist, Hairdresser and so on to help her keep on top of the job.

You may later be involved in planning transport, speeches, listing gifts the bride receives, plans for supervising children, and giving honeymoon advice. Don't take the bride's wedding decisions for her, but be available to escort her. You might offer, 'Monday is my day off. I can drive you, if you like.'

STATIONERY

Order floral or decorative stationery suitable for writing thank-you cards. You may be asked to help with writing invitations and placecards, too, unless the bride employs professional calligraphers and printed cards. Look at lace-trimmed wedding cards at stationers and printers, and help the bride plan the order of service and music. Cassettes of wedding music are available from music stores.

COMPUTERISED INVITATIONS AND CARDS

There are computer programmes which design individualised greeting cards in black on white paper or in colour if you have a colour printer. Such programmes can be used on compatible personal computers.

Computer graphics programmes can also create designs such as outsize hearts. Fold them to make heart-shaped cards, or stick cut-out hearts inside a card on horizontally cut folds to make pop-up designs. Outsize cards can be made using a colour photocopying machine which expands the picture size. It is fun experimenting to make a card to present to the bride at a hen party, invitations to surprise parties, a personalised thank you card, or an anniversary card. Small numbers of cards are fun to make and embellish with silver sprinkles, bits of net and lacy ribbon. Personalise invitations with silver writing and borders, spray-on glitter, silver stars, miniature plastic bags of confetti, stick on confetti, or a foil-wrapped chocolate (not in hot weather). Visit Christmas and party shops for ideas. Attach tokens such as silver shoes from cake decorating shops.

For a hundred or more invitations you need grander and less time-consuming cards. Specialized business promotion companies make individual theme designs with pop-up centres, cake, bride and groom, church.

PLACECARDS

Experiment with fibre tip pens or, better, a fountain pen and inexpensive white paper. For placecards use wide oblongs of glossy card. To make a projecting heart draw the heart in colour centrally. Rule a horizontal line half way up outside the heart. Cut the outline of the top half of the heart above the line. Fold the card in half horizontally along the pencil line without folding the heart. Write neatly inside the heart the name of the person who sits there. The wedding date and name of bride and groom can be added in the corner.

SHOPPING

GIFTS

The Groom's Gift

For the man who always considers himself last when buying presents, buy what he needs. The bride can find what he would like. If the groom is a student, you could buy smart clothes for his new office job, a matching shirt and tie, jumper, jacket, personal organizer, or expanding briefcase.

For the man who has everything, you could always follow his sporting interests. There are many accessories or gifts specially for golfers, footballers, fishermen, and so on. Another idea that would be appreciated is a watch. Co-ordinated 'his and hers' watches are available or you could have a design created especially for him. For the practical type, or one who should be more practical, how about a Swiss army knife?

PAGEBOY'S AND JUNIOR BRIDESMAID'S GIFTS

In the UK the groom traditionally buys presents for the ushers and best man. The bride might be asked for advice or be delegated the shopping by a busy groom, especially if she is buying for the pageboys. The smallest children might like a watch decorated with a cartoon character or the latest hero craze.

The traditional gold or silver bracelet loses its novelty for a small girl who has already been a bridesmaid. However, a charm bracelet allows her to add charms each time. Visit children's shops or use their mail order catalogues.

GIFTS FOR CHILD BRIDEMAIDS

Jewellers sell name necklaces, matching necklace, bracelet and ring sets in silver, and charm bracelets with teddy bear motifs or rocking horses.

GIFTS TO ADULT BRIDESMAIDS

The bride chooses a gift, ideally engraved with the wedding cake or the initials of the recipient. Identical gifts should be given to prevent jealousy unless ages make it impractical. The maid of honour and the best man get larger gifts. Traditional choices are items of value in gold or silver, a heart-shape locket, pendant with charm representing a thimble, scissors (for hairdressers), cat, dog, ballerina, opening boot, saxophone, drum and guitar, darts, ice skate, and football, brooch, compact with light, illuminated make-up mirror, musical jewel box, embroidered jewellery case, engraved picture frame, luggage or clock. Inexpensive silver sets of matching necklace and ear-rings are available. Pick a perfume she likes but cannot afford, a

silk scarf, failing all else a gift certificate from her favourite shop.

The older matron of honour who has a home might appreciate a tray, silver candlesticks, a silver religious item or picnic set.

GIFTS TO THE BRIDE AT ENGAGEMENT AND SHOWER PARTIES

The bride might like a ring-minder for the kitchen or bedroom. Silver or gold charm bracelets are suitable. Add charms representing church, opening bible, bride and groom, stork, and I love you.

GIFTS TO BRIDE AND GROOM FROM BRIDESMAIDS

Various shops supply cushions with jokey messages including, 'I'm not perfect but I'm perfect for you', 'If you ever leave me I'm going with you', 'Marriages are made in heaven. So is thunder and lightening', and 'Behind every successful marriage there's a surprised mother-in-law'. For the second marriage perhaps, 'Eat drink and remarry,' or 'Older men make better lovers'. These sayings can also be inscribed on pill/pin boxes.

Brides not employing a photographer, who normally sells an album as part of the package, might like a wedding album. Silver-plated and heart-shape photograph frames are also available.

Large toy and games departments in major stores sell backgammon, playing card sets and green baize table-cloth marked with cards. For the couple who have everything, consider unusual furniture such as a card-table, rocking chair or hammock. Perhaps best of all, ask what they want.

GIFTS TO BRIDE'S AND GROOM'S PARENTS

Find old family wedding photos. If you find a suitable one you could have it copied, retouched and framed for the bride's mother or mother-in-law as well as, or instead of, the usual bouquet at the wedding reception. A bridesmaid who is the groom's sister can organize this for the bride as a gift to the groom's family.

GIFT WRAPPING

Don't forget to remove the price before wrapping the gift! To enable the recipient to change the gift leave the price on a book jacket, or enclose the bill in a sealed envelope passed to the recipient's mother. French shops automatically wrap gifts at no extra cost. Some shops gift-wrap for a small charge.

Checklist – Shopping
Bridal doll sources: ....
toy supplier tel: ....
Menswear shops for groom's gifts: ....
Ladies wear shops for trousseau: ....
Jewellers: ....
Health club address: ....
Department store with wedding list: Name, address, phone ....
Shopping List:
Keepbook; Ostrich plume pen for signing register; Wedding reception guests autograph album; other .....
Obtain lucky symbols: silver colour horseshoe or real horseshoe, or cardboard lucky black cat; buy silver sixpence or threepence from coin shop or have five pence handy for bride's shoe; four-leaf clover; organize lucky chimney sweep.

ARRANGING ACCOMMODATION

The bride tries to give accommodation in her house to the chief bridesmaid and the immediate family or friends who cannot afford hotels. For those who want the hotel comforts, and don't wish to impose on the bride's family, she can find out the availability of hotel accommodation and make a booking on her guests' behalf. The chief bridesmaid may offer accommodation to other bridesmaids, or meet and greet them, seeing them to their hotel.

BOOKING ACCOMMODATION

If ten or more guests are staying in the same hotel you probably qualify for a group rate. In any case, you have opportunity for bargaining and upgrading the bride to the best accommodation such as seaview room.

Budget accommodation can be obtained from hotels offering weekend breaks. Obtain accommodation directories for hotel groups and make reservations cost free using freephone numbers. 'Tollfree' means for the cost of a local call you contact companies' central reservation systems booking their hotels worldwide.

Some hotels have a 'kids to stay free' policy which allows two children such as the bridesmaid and pageboy to stay in their parents' room without further charge. Other hotels charge by the room enabling up to four bridesmaids to share accommodation.

Airport and city centre hotel with shuttle bus services save the family from waiting in arrival lounges for delayed planes.

A few hotels offer a packing and unpacking service. This enables you to go out for drinks on the last evening and let the hotel do the chore. Check whether you can book this service for the bride.

If the bride-to-be needs to go down to the hotel bar or household lounge to meet distant relatives, speed progress by unpacking for her. Several bridesmaids can adopt a relay system. The chief bridesmaid hands clothes from the suitcase to the others and gives instructions. One bridesmaid takes items for the wardrobe, hanging up dresses and the bridal gown, and pairing shoes. Another folds lingerie and blouses in the drawers. The little bridesmaid or pageboy carries toothbrushes and toiletry bag into the bathroom. Four of you can finish in five minutes a task which would take the bride twenty. Big hotels loan irons or offer a pressing service within 24 hours, sometimes same day. Steaming may be required, rather than risking ironing the lace.

BEAUTY TREATMENTS

Exercising and Dieting Together
Share exercising and dieting together, or perhaps visits to a health club, aerobics classes, swimming, sunbed treatments or a suntanning holiday. The bride could visit a health and beauty club for the day, perhaps as an engagement gift from the chief bridesmaid. Spend a day together dieting every weekend.

No time or will power? Spend a weekend or day at a health farm. It might be fun (and useful too) to attend a lecture by a colour consultant. They select a member of the audience, hold colours to her face and chose the range of colours which suit her best. For a fee, the colour consultant selects your colours and gives you a swatch to match when buying clothes, so bride and bridesmaids can reorganise their entire wardrobe.

Beauticians can do a pre-wedding make-up consultation colour analysis, tint eyelashes and brows, shape brows, and on the day make up the bride and three bridesmaids.

For spots and sores zinc ointment avaiable from chemists is a skin soother. Natural products and caffeine-free herbal teas are sold by health shops. Various preparations claim to help acne, calm nerves and provide vitamins needed when taking the contraceptive pill. Ask your doctor's and pharmacist's advice.

DENTAL TREATMENT

Missing, broken, crooked, stained or discoloured teech can ruin that perfect wedding smile. Visit the dental hygienist for advice and treatment.

STOP SMOKING

Join the bride in attempting to give up smoking. Avoid being photographed holding a cigarette at the wedding, and don't blow smoke over newly-washed hair or clothes which need dry cleaning.

HAIRSTYLE

Hair should not be too flowing in church completely covering the dress so that you look as if you are naked underneath like Lady Godiva. Long tresses can be held back neatly with flowers. Try the chosen hairstyle the week before, taking the hair adornment to the hairdresser. Some hairdressers will do your hair and manicures at home. Don't surprise the bride by turning from brunette to blonde. Apart from anything else, it can alter the colours which suit you.

BEAUTY SLEEP

Allow time to recover from jet-lag after a long plane journey. Apart from feeling exhausted you look haggard until sufficient sleep restores your schoolgirl complexion and white eyes. Have an early night before the wedding day. If you share a room with the bride and she is too excited to sleep, walk her up and down until she is tired.

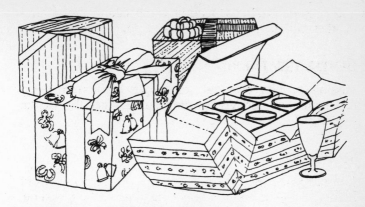

Checklist – Health and beauty

Have all the bridesmaids' hair done by the same hairdresser.

Doctor's name, address and phone: ....

Dentist's name, address and phone: ....

Family Planning address, tel: ....

Bride's appointment date and time ....

    Does bride want a companion? ....

Health Club address and tel: ....

Class dates, times, costs ....

Hairdresser's name, address and phone ....

    apointment date and time .... Assistant ....

Checklist

Packing:

Dress(es) .... Hat .... Shoes......... Hosiery ....

Underclothes .... Outdoor clothes .... Swimwear ......

Cosmetics bag .... Toiletries/medicaments bag ....

Dictionary .... Passport .... Address list ....

Gifts .... Tickets ....

Speeches and music .... Camera ....

Instruction book ....

Film ... Batteries ... Mail order developing envelope ....

Other ....

PARTY PLANNING AND SPEECHES

An event as important as a marriage need not be celebrated with merely one party alone – a reception – there are many other opportunities to celebrate the event, and you can help to organize them.

ENGAGEMENT PARTY AND WEDDING VENUES

The bride usually chooses her wedding reception venue (and sometimes the engagement party) from local hotels, village and church halls. You can also entertain in a private room at a restaurant, hotel or at home. In case she asks for advice here are more ideas. Check local guildhalls, medical centres or halls connected with the families' work. The engagement party is often arranged at short notice. Wedding reception venues, like churches, get booked up over a year in advance for summer, so rapid fact-finding and decision-making are essential.

If the bride asks for help in choosing a venue, you could investigate unusual museums, the zoo, or whether there are private function rooms at public buildings. In general, unusual venues are more appropriate for engagement parties, and grand hotels and castles are better for more formal wedding receptions. Wherever you live in the world, once you start looking for venues you will be surprised at the wide choice available.

PARTY PREPARATION

The bride's parents may decide to hold a seated dinner for relatives travelling long distances to meet the couple. A young people's party is often held at the bride's home. The bride's sister or best friend helps with a party held at home. The bride's sister probably already expects to be a bridesmaid. Your dress sense and help with decorating and catering at the engagement party may convince the bride she must have you!

Good stationers sell sets of balloons with messages such as Congratulations, or Happy Engagement. For a toast to the happy couple serve champagne, a champagne cocktail, or a sparkling wine.

ENGAGEMENT PARTY CLOTHES

For a formal engagement party such as a dance at a grand hotel ballroom you can buy or hire evening gowns. With an evening dress in black and blue or black and red you might wear matching long black gloves and black shoes. For an afternoon party you might wear a sophisticated Italian pink dress with matching pink hat, gloves, shoes and handbag, all one colour. If you want a secondary contrasting colour, accessories should co-ordinate. It is simplest to match black accessories for winter evenings, white for summer, silver or gold if you have silver and gold evening shoes. Satin shoes can be dyed one colour or mottled to match a dress.

Checklist – Engagement party
Engagement party location: Name, address, phone ....
contact .... date .... time ....
Engagement party date .... time ....

Engagement party guest numbers invited ....
Engagement party guest numbers accepted ....
Possible engagement and wedding venues ....
Nearest company hiring static boats and trains ....
Chosen venue ....
Musicians ....
Caterer ....
Gown hire shop ....
Dry cleaners tel .... opening hours ....
   time needed for cleaning ....
   collection date ....
Nearly new designer clothes shop ....
Bride-to-be's clothes .... shoes ....
   handbag..................... coat ....
My clothes ....; shoes ....; handbag ....; coat ....

THE HEN PARTY

The hen party is the bride's last fling, a girls' night out
with no-one expecting her home to cook dinner or
account for her whereabouts. The bridesmaids often
organize the hen party at a date close to the wedding,
usually a lunch or evening event. But at a weekend they
could start in a single sex sauna or leisure centre,
whirlpool bath, return home for simple entertainment
such as listening to cassettes and admiring wedding
gifts, or go out to a club or dinner.

Plan in advance any announcements, speeches, thanks
you don't want to forget, and photographs you may wish
to take. Organize transport sharing cars so the bride-to-
be does not have to drive.

ENTERTAINING IN HOTEL SUITES

At all-suite hotels each main bedroom also has a sitting
room usually containing a fridge-bar and sink, and
sometimes a microwave. This helps economise on meals

and drinks, providing you don't consume too much hotel-price alcohol. Use the room to entertain, hold a hen party, or reciprocate invitations from the bride's family.

LIVE ENTERTAINMENT

You might attend a medieval banquet at a stately home. Ask banquet entertainment organisers if there are souvenir records or cassettes of the evening which the girls can buy for the bride-to-be. Tell the organizers in advance that she is in the audience so she can be called out as a 'volunteer' for games. They might seat her in a place of honour with a good view near the front, convenient for a singer to come forward from the stage to sing to her, or for her to be called on stage. If your guests need special diets or are teetotallers, warn the caterers.

GIFTS

Find out the bride's interests and choose something appropriate. For example, for someone who takes vitamin pills, a pill box, for someone who is always late, an alarm watch, for someone who wears lots of jewellery a jewel case. Visitors books with a quotation on the left page and lines for names and addresses are another idea – or why not give the bride-to-be a book about a Royal Wedding?

PARTYING AT HOME

If the party is to be held at a house, it might be fun to organise a pink party and a pink cake containing a symbol such as a ring, thimble or lucky charm – an omen that whoever finds it will be the next bride.

Play party games adapted to the wedding theme, *e.g.*

wedding crosswords; wedding Scrabble; wedding bingo (Bride's bingo is sold in America); unscrambling words (names of wedding group as well as marriage-related items); pin the carnation on the groom; pin the bouquet on the bride; where will she wear the ring?

MUSIC FOR A HEN PARTY

Records and songbooks will give you the words of songs such as Jolly Good Company, The More We Are Together. Or you can have a guessing game, playing the first bar of the tune, and the guests have to guess the name, who, what, or where. Use songs with the bridesmaids', bride's, ushers' and groom's names, for example, 'Oh no John, no John, no John, no!', or 'When Johnny Comes Marching Home Again', or play around with placename songs such as 'Sweet Lass of Richmond Hill'.

You can string songs together to tell a story with a compere or narrator, beginning with the fact that the engaged couple are rushing into marriage, or have known each other so long that you wondered whether they would ever make up their minds. You could have a chorus singing the verse from a well-known song such as the music hall number 'Daisy, Daisy', using the tune everybody knows but adapting the words, 'Will she, won't she, give me your answer do!'

TRANSPORT

Groom and ushers or boyfriends should be briefed to arrive at the end to admire gifts and give girls lifts home. Alternatively call taxis, or pay a cab to make a round trip delivering all the girls, ending at the home of the chief bridesmaid so that she is last to alight and pays the fare.

Checklist – Parties

Who is tidying, clearing up, rearranging furniture? ....

Washing up? ....

Returning attendants clothes? ....

Returning cake and leftover food and drink? ....

Returning wedding gift display? ....

Entertaining late-night revellers? ....

Organising transport? ....

Providing beds? ....

Who is up early next day to let in workmen collecting
    the marquee? ....

Who makes breakfast/brunch the morning after, and
    lunch or dinner? ....

PREPARING SPEECHES

HEN PARTY SPEECH

At a hen party you won't make a formal speech from pages of notes but you might like to stand up and make what appear to be a few spontaneous comments – but which you will have practised a little beforehand. Start with an amusing line like, 'I always thought that "A bachelor girl is a girl looking for a bachelor"' and relate it to the subject of your speech 'and now that Anne has found Marc ...' and make a comment on behalf of yourself or the company 'but I/we think, Anne, that you should know ...'

For other suggestions see *Wedding Speeches & Toasts* published in this series. If you choose to make a speech, keep it personal but not offensive, and make sure you do not speak for too long and slow up the party.

OTHER IDEAS

You can buy a hardback book like a scrapbook with quotations and famous paintings illustrating each stage in the engagement and wedding, courtship, proposal, honeymoon, with space for the bride to fill in where hers took place and add a photo.

Or you could create a home-makers book for the bride containing recipes in minutes, tips, and goodwill messages from everyone. In a small autograph book visitors will write traditional verses such as, 'I wish you health, I wish you wealth, I wish you gold in store, I wish you heaven when you die, What could I wish you more.' Old cliches might be new to a young bride. But to prevent people repeating identical verses suggest they vary them with original phrases relevant to the wedding in question.

One idea that has proved popular is to present a home-made marriage book: Collect top tips for a happy marriage from all guests during the meal, circulating a guests' autograph book. Warn guests in advance so they prepare something. Find a translator and someone with good handwriting to write on behalf of any foreign guests.

Or give everyone a slip of paper which you staple in a wedding album or place in a book with adhesive see-through pages. You could present it to the bride and groom at the end of the reception.

HELPING WITH WEDDING SPEECHES

You may possibly be asked to call for speeches, help the bride with her speech if she is to make one, or describe the modest bride's virtues to the best man. Ensure he doesn't tell rude jokes; try personalizing the speech, or writing a poem about how the bride and groom met. At some weddings the chief bridesmaid has even made a joint speech with the best man, alternating comments on the bride and groom.

Speeches frequently include compliments to the bridesmaids, with such phrases as, 'They have helped to make this a memorable day,'. During a speech about you the guests and video camera may be watching you. Do not look down. Look at the speaker. Smile briefly in modest acknowledgement if you are complimented by name but still keep your head up. When glasses are raised in a toast to you, the bridesmaids, do not lift your glass or stand up.

THE WEDDING

All those hours of planning come to fruition on the big day – but your priority must be to stay alert and help the bride look and feel her best.

THE WEDDING REHEARSAL

A rehearsal is helpful and usually takes place the day before the wedding. A rehearsal usually takes place in church to familiarize attendants with where to enter, order in the procession and recession, distance apart and speed of walking, and where to stand during the ceremony. You need to practice mounting steps and carrying the train, perhaps with a stand-in wearing a white paper imitation train. Watching another wedding from pews the previous week is helpful, but does not give you the same confidence as actually standing in position.

The wedding rehearsal could be held the night before the ceremony. A dress rehearsal is useful so attendants can practice walking in long dresses. Wear shoes and correct pinching using shoe stretch liquid if necessary. Try on the head-dress to be sure it won't slip off. You may need pins to hold it.

Check underclothes. Prevent bra straps slipping off shoulders or peeping above the neckline of the dress, dark underclothes showing through light dresses, tight underwear making lines across the back of the skirt, loose hems catching high heels, and small size tights splitting as you put them on or getting snagged by jewellery.

A rehearsal dinner or bridesmaids' and ushers' dinner can be held for out-of-town members of the wedding party to meet each other and be entertained. Remember that guests might also like time for shopping and sight-seeing. If the bride's family are busy, book guests tickets for an open top bus tour and meet for a late tea, dinner or buffet supper. Discuss the receiving line positions.

PREPARATIONS

If you are attending a morning ceremony followed by a wedding breakfast you must be up early. Run a bath for the bride and if required drive her to the hairdresser. The chief bridesmaid should dress herself and help dress younger bridesmaids and the bride. This may entail hairstyling and manicure, or retouching a chipped or broken nail if the manicure has been done the day before. When the fresh flower circlet is delivered sew it to the bride's veil. Clean the bride's engagement ring with an old toothbrush. Remove price tags from the base of new shoes so they don't show when she is kneeling in church. Supply concealer cream for last minute spots. Calm the bride's mother if necessary.

Be ready in time for the photographer who will photograph the bride alone, also with the maid of honour, then the bridesmaids. Beware: the video camera may find you all dressing in your underslips pulling on dresses and zipping them up! You may wish to remove wires normally used to straighten teeth.

If the reception is held at home before leaving for church check the marquee to see that the placecards are ready.

TRANSPORT

The bride rides to church alongside her father driven by a chauffeur. The bride's mother drives herself or travels with a family friend. The bridesmaid's father drives her from her home. When several bridesmaids travel with the bride's mother from the bride's family home it is worthwhile hiring a second car. If bridesmaids are the bride's sisters you can use one stretch limousine for the whole family. These and other long wheelbase vehicles are roomy enough to seat several bridesmaids with plenty of space for long dresses.

Don't order cars with tinted windows or windows which wind only half way down. You want to be seen and photographed. A chauffeur-driven car may have a barrier between driver and passengers (like a taxi) whereas some limousines are designed to be owner-driven and have open interiors. A best man or friend driving will not want to be separate. The grandest cars have air conditioning, cocktail bars, radio or TV sets in the back. The chauffeur should alight to open the car doors for you.

The same car can transport bridesmaids to the bride's home, to church, and on to the reception. Technically the groom pays for transport to the reception but it is simpler to have one car if the ceremony is brief if, say, it is at a register office. Traditionally bridesmaids travel to church separately from the bride in order to arrive ahead, wait and greet her in the porch. If you are all in one car, the chief bridesmaid should hop out first to help her fellow passengers.

If the bride's mother isn't travelling with you be prepared to direct the driver to the church door or register office car park. Know the route from the church to the reception hotel or back to the bride's home. Carry the church and reception addresses and phone numbers.

The best man might drive the groom to the church or register office. If the groom takes his own car to drive off on honeymoon, the best man may drive the bridesmaids. At church the best man should wait until last so that he can check for gloves left behind. Later, another car, perhaps the chief usher's, takes the bridesmaids from church to the reception.

If the church is less than 10 minutes away the car can make a first trip with the bridesmaids and a second with the bride. The bridesmaids will not want to be kept waiting for the bride more than 20 minutes. A limousine seating seven is an ideal second car.

Etiquette is supposed to keep everybody happy, not upset them. One pageboy aged about five tried to climb into a grand carriage with the bride and when removed burst into tears. So the kind bride said, 'Never mind. Let him ride with us'.

Checklist – Transport

Bridal car(s): Rolls Royce, Daimler, Mercedes, saloon/ limousine ....

Number of bridesmaids to seat ....

Motorcade: car colours ....

Information from motoring organisations tel: ....

Bridesmaids' journey to bride's home: Bridesmaids' return ....
    train/flight/taxi from: Location address and phone ....
    date .... time ....

Journey from bride's home ....

Taxi company name, address and phone ....

Arrival date and time ....

Return from reception .... to ....

Car company: .... tel: ....

Model of bridal car to church ....
    year of numberplate ....
    colour of car .... ribbon colour ....
    flowers .... umbrella ....

Arrival time .... replacement car in event of breakdown ....

Time of departure from bride's home ....

Parking place while waiting at church ....

Car to reception arrives at church at time ....

    departs from church time ...... arrives at reception ......

red carpet .... doorman .... changing room ....

meeting point for toastmaster/master of ceremonies ....

Going away car ....; holder of car keys ....

decorating going away car ....

BEING PHOTOGRAPHED

As a bridesmaid you are right at the centre of things – and that means getting used to the unblinking eye of the camera! In group photographs the bride's sister stands nearer the bride and groom than distant relatives. Tiny pages and bridesmaids stand or sit in front so they can be seen. On steps outside the church and inside the reception hall or hotel, the bride stands at the top of the steps and the bridesmaid drapes the bride's train down the steps.

Fetch a champagne glass so the bride can be photographed as if raising the glass for a toast. Arrange the bride's dress. The train is usually draped in front of her so it can be seen in the photograph, and you should spread her skirt on the staircase in fan shape. If required, you could help and call guests as they are to be photographed. The bride is photographed with child attendants, then all attendants.

Bridesmaids who have not removed their glasses for the procession might do so for photographs. It is usual to photograph bridesmaids individually, chief bridesmaid and best man, bridesmaids with ushers, child bridesmaids with their parents, bridesmaids with their boyfriends, and the matron of honour with her husband. A traditional group photograph of bridesmaids shows them revealing garters.

TAKING PHOTOGRAPHS

You have so much to do that you may be best advised to lend your camera to a friend to take photographs – that way you can be in the pictures too! However you may be able to step to one side and take some snaps yourself. Carry extra film in case your camera jams or someone forgets film and needs more. Take photographs of the hotel name, the wording on the cake and the car with numberplate. These shots make opening credits in an album and help identify film if it is lost by processors. Don't forget to carry spare batteries.

POSES TO CHOOSE

To create height for a bride and groom with taller attendants have the bride and groom standing on a doorstep, attendants stand either side, ushers with one leg raised onto the step. Arrange the poses of junior attendants. A page might pose with his hand in his belt, cap in hand, or hold his hat under his arm.

Indoors to avoid red eyes under flashlight have another light source from windows or turn on more lights. The subjects should not all stare at the camera. The bride and groom can look at each other.

Prevent flashlight whitening the faces by keeping about five feet distant. Check your camera instruction book and practise in advance.

If the photos are not successful you may be able to

photograph the bride and bridesmaids in bridal clothes a few days later. If hired clothes must be returned photograph the bride with a veil or flowers in her hair alongside the groom, or alone beside a lighted candle or candelabra.

Early this century, photographs often showed the bride and groom seated together, the whole group seated, or the bride and groom standing with bridesmaids seated and ushers or taller bridesmaids standing behind. Some such formal shots are still usually taken (though not often with seating), and photographers often take some more relaxed pictures too.

Sit elegantly, either ankles crossed and toes together, or knees together and ankles to one side, or knees, ankles and toes together in front of you. Sit up staight. Don't block the view of the person behind or hide behind the person in front. Don't look worried. Smile and try not to spread your mouth in a false artificial grin showing lots of teeth with unsmiling eyes.

VIDEOTAPING

Photographs can be taken from videotapes and photographs can be made up into a videotape for showing on a screen, perhaps as the opening title shot.

Videotape companies can arrive at the bride's house before the wedding and show the bridesmaids helping the bride to dress and adjusting their own hair and make-up. Everything you say is enshrined on the tape forever unless edited out, so be careful not to insult others, nor order them about, nor to look peeved or indecisive.

The bride may order a more expensive video package involving more than one camera. During the ceremony, particularly long services using foreign languages, while the priest is speaking the video often focuses on bridesmaids taking close-up of faces by zooming in and out. Look attentive. Don't giggle and hold up your hand and whisper behind your glove to other bridesmaids, or stare vacantly into space with your mouth open, or bite your lips anxiously and sniff, or frown and pull the corner of your mouth to one side.

Food is usually provided for the videotaping team, but you may like to check that they are happy with it, as the bride is obviously unable to take on this role.

The video makers may pass a microphone along the top table and get each of the ushers and bridesmaids in turn to say a few words to the bride and groom, usually variations on, 'Congratulations to Mike and Sue. It's been a lovely wedding. I hope you have a beautiful honeymoon in Greece and a wonderful long and happy married life together.' Alternatively the film-makers may stop you when you are dancing, or get you to raise a glass and add a message at the end of the film just after the bride and groom have driven off.

When leaving the ceremony area or entering the reception area any toddlers may have to be helped down the steps. This is easiest if the bridesmaid is assisted by another bridesmaid or an usher.

Checklist – At the church.

While you wait at the church before the ceremony keep neat and tidy and occupy other bridesmaids during the wait for the bride outside the church.

Go to the toilet with junior bridesmaids. (Send pageboys under age of seven to toilet with an usher.)

Comb hair. Check shoes and clothes.

Blow noses of small bridesmaids and pageboys.

Pay compliments to other bridesmaids, especially juniors.

Point out the exit door and where you will stand for photographs afterwards.

Supervise younger bridesmaids.

In the procession walk ahead of the bride behind younger bridesmaids.

Take the bouquet from the bride at the start of the ceremony.

Sign the register as witness.

Return the bouquet after the signing of the register/after the ceremony.

In the recession walk with the best man behind the bride.

Travel ahead of the bride to the reception and arrange her dress for photographs.

At most church weddings the organist strikes up with Here Comes The Bride or other music to warn the congregation of the bride's arrival. For a grand effect a trumpet fanfare announces her arrival so that those seated in the congregation stand up.

THE CEREMONY

Procession Order

In the procession sometimes the vicar, priest or rabbi leads. The page or ring bearer is followed by the flower girl. Decide whether they are likely to behave better hand-in-hand, or less likely to fight and pull in opposite directions if separated with one following the other. The maid of honour precedes the matron of honour, then come the ring bearer, flower girl, junior bridesmaid.

Jewish American option: 1 Ushers 2 Bridesmaids 3 Maid of honour 4 Ring bearer 5 Flower girl 6 Bride's father and bride.

At one wedding, an older bride without a living father chose to walk up the aisle on the arm of her matron of honour who, however, did not hand the bride over. During the service the vicar simply stated, 'I give this woman ...' and handed the bride to the groom.

THE MARRIAGE

The maid of honour or chief bridesmaid stands behind the bride holding bouquet and prayerbook, and wearing the bride's engagement ring unless the bride wears it on her right hand. The ring can be returned after signing the register out of sight or just before entering the reception.

The junior bridesmaid could hold the bride's gloves during the ceremony and in a two-ring ceremony the groom's ring. If the bride has gloves without fingers or has made a slit in the seams of the glove's ring finger this will not be necessary.

In an Anglican church the best man hands the ring to the vicar who blesses it and then gives it to the groom. The best man signals with a slight wave of his hand to the chief bridesmaid that she can retire and she enters the pew to sit down. Move small bridesmaids ahead into the pew so they don't skip down the aisle to join their mother.

SIGNING THE REGISTER

If the chief bridesmaid is a witness she follows the bride into the vestry and returns the bouquet to the bride in the vestry after the bride has signed the register. Otherwise she stays where she is, and organizes her colleagues for the recession.

To arrange the train for the recession, the bridesmaid may have to place her own bouquet on the table, hand it to the bride's mother, or put it on the floor and retrieve it later.

While the congregation waits often music plays, a choir sings, and the entire congregation joins in the hymns.

THE RECESSION

The Recession order is the reverse of the procession with the bride first instead of last.

1 bride and groom 2 ring bearer 3 flower girl 4 maid

of honour 5 bridesmaid(s) 6 ushers.

The chief bridesmaid is paired with the best man in the recession.

Or: 1 bride and groom 2 flower girl plus ring bearer 3 junion bridesmaids) or pages, then older or taller bridesmaid last.

Don't tread on the bride's train or dress. Watch that the bride doesn't twirl around a corner, toss her head and catch her long veil on a post, as one bride did. The bridesmaid saved the day by reaching forward, and disentangled it so quickly that the bride never noticed. You really have to stay alert!

AFTERWARDS

Confetti
Ask in advance if the bride wants confetti so she isn't disappointed by its absence. If it rains she might prefer not to risk getting coloured patches on her white dress. When guests throw confetti, rice or birdseed you may have as much confetti thrown over you as over the bride. When pelted by rice which is quite hard you have to shake it out of your dress.

The flower girl might also present a posy to the bride just before her departure.

At the reception venue, the chief bridesmaid goes with the bride to the bedroom suite or changing room and has a comb for the bride, lipstick, and hanky, then helps the bride downstairs to join the receiving line.

SECOND MARRIAGE

Plan food, entertainment and babysitting afterwards even for granny's small wedding. One elderly couple

went back to their family's house and ended up babysitting both sets of grandchildren while the children went shopping.

HANDICAPPED PARTICIPANTS

You may be involved in helping any handicapped people in various ways on the big day – this can add a satisfying new dimension to the joyous celebrations as you help them share the event.

BLIND BRIDAL PARTY

A blind or partially sighted bride may need help from

the bridesmaid when dressing, but she may have many clever ideas such as putting string through the zip, enabling her to zip her own dress up. Visually impaired bridesmaids may also require extra assistance with dressing.

The blind bride will be on her father's arm and groom's arm so the ceremony will present few difficulties except with steps on entering the building. Check whether buildings such as the reception venue and/or the hotel have special provisions and advise the bride. Some hotels have lifts with floor numbers marked in braille and bedroom doors with braille numbers.

The majority of blind people are over 65 so you are more likely to be helping the bride's grandmother and older relatives than the bride herself. Few people who become partially sighted in later life can read braille and large print invitations are more useful. Arrange to meet them outside buildings to help them enter. Show them to the bathroom on the way in.

At home clear overhanging branches from paths. Indoors move toys and obstacles off the floor and keep doors shut or wide open. At a buffet reception collect food and drink for blind and partially-sighted people. Introduce them to others at standing room only receptions, and locate relatives they want to meet and cannot see.

DEAF PARTICIPANTS

Even if you know sign language, it is a good idea to have an interpreter translating into sign language at the speed of speech. The interpreter should attend the practice or wedding rehearsal and go to pre-wedding consultations to get everything agreed by the vicar or priest. A vicar who won't normally allow video-recording might make an exception after realising how much the deaf miss without aural memory of hymns, songs and speech.

You might like to make a detailed order of service including the words of hymns, timing from the entry of the bride onwards, name the bridal march which deaf people won't hear and identify, and mention that an interpreter will be signing. One bride whose groom was deaf used sign language when making her vows.

Hearing bridesmaids chosen from the family of the deaf bride or groom can be very helpful. The bride may have her veil lifted by her father so her lips can be seen so the deaf groom and guests can see her and lipread.

In a large church the interpreter should stand high up so the signing can be seen by deaf people at the back. At one wedding where half the guests had hearing difficulties most of the deaf people sat on the side of the church facing the interpreter while all the hearing people sat the other side. The interpreter followed the photographer to summon deaf people to be photographed and instructed them how to be grouped and when to smile.

The bride's family usually choose their family church for the wedding, unless a church for the deaf is nearby, although several special churches for the deaf exist.

Churches for the deaf are smaller so that everyone can see, and have fewer pillars obscuring vision, front-facing seats, and soundproofing to reduce traffic noise and echoes from people walking up the aisle. The vicar and staff may be deaf and can use sign language. The standard choir is often supplemented by a group using sign language.

You could make a special effort to teach ushers the fingerspell alphabet so that they can give the bride's and groom's names, 'Jane, or John?' when asking guests where they want to sit.

To help others lipread face them and speak clearly keeping your head still. When you are not understood don't shout which distorts your face but try again using different words.

In restaurants deaf people can communicate by pointing at the menu and carrying a card which says, 'I am deaf but can lipread. Please stand facing the light and don't have the light behind you.' This is useful when making introductions at the wedding reception.

WHEELCHAIR USERS

Access causes the most difficulties for wheelchair users – especially steps. Brief two ushers to help in getting wheelchairs inside buildings. Order one of the modern taxis which are adapted with space on the left beside the driver to allow room for a wheelchair.

Many hotels have adapted ground floor bedrooms where you can stay overnight or use bathroom facilities during the reception and ramps into dining rooms. At a buffet be on hand to delegate someone else to supply food to guests who cannot move about. Make sure that wheelchairs can be fitted under the reception tables. Have photographs taken of the bride and bridesmaids seated with wheelchair-bound guests behind the table so that they are not obviously different nor seated while others stand towering above.

The video can be shown to the wheelchair-bound guests afterwards so they can see what went on in parts of the building such as the garden where they could not go.

At church help family members using crutches to the front pew in advance, even the bride's mother who normally enters last. Check whether nearer side doors are open.

TROUBLESHOOTING GUIDANCE

Your jobs include asking about possible problems and having backup plans, finding missing items or supplying duplicates, opening bottles and locks, repairing and mending, fetching and returning items, and sending thanks. Stock a bag containing: pen, notebook, glue, scissors, coins for phone boxes, phonecard, paper tissues, spare tights, taxi phone number, nail varnish and remover, comb, lipstick, handcream, spotcover, perfume, disposable toothbrush and toothpaste, pocket clothes brush or lint remover, Swiss army knife containing bottle-opener, nailfile, mini-scissors and tweezers, camera film, batteries, non-aspirin painkiller, elastoplast/band-aid, attendants' medication, sanitary towels, spare car keys, dictionary, diary, address-telephone book containing phone numbers of nearest doctor, airport, and railway station, cards with your business, home and hotel addresses for guests to contact you afterwards, hair rollers, hair drier, travel iron, moisturiser, Waspeze, zinc ointment, first aid kit, shoe-cleaning wipes, suntan oil and sunburn lotion (in hot countries).

This bag can be left in the changing room provided by the church or hotel, or in the boot of a car for which you have keys.

When the bride spills red wine on her dress and is about to burst into tears what will you do? Ask dress suppliers about stain removal in advance. If the dress is home-made or custom-made take a spare piece of material and try dropping red and white wine on it and test the action of stain removers. Carry notes on removing confetti and wine stains, such as how to remove red wine using salt or white wine, removing stains of confetti colours running in rain, or removing grass stains. Prevention is better than cure.

Swap dresses if the vicar won't marry the bride in her red dress or a miniskirt. Or drive home for a long skirt or coat.

Make friends of hotel staff in advance. In hotels catering disasters such as sinking cakes, food shortages, and guests on diets, can be sorted out by hotel staff. Avoid drinking too much, and convert to low alcohol after your third drink or add more mixers each time. Watch known alcoholics and ask waiters not to keep refilling their glasses with neat alcohol.

Repair tears in wedding dress or clothing. For needles and cotton try the staffed ladies cloakroom, housekeeping department, guest relations, reception, and if no luck phone the hotel manager. If the groom dances on the bride's dress and splits the skirt and she says he is a 'clumsy, careless ...' and the groom retorts that she has chosen a stupid impractical dress and they are about to have a row, you can save the day. Try joking, 'Now, now, children. He's made sure you won't be able to wear that again,' separation and distraction, 'John, your mother wants to see you ...' and, 'Never mind, Anne. Come upstairs and I'll sew on some spare ribbon. No-one will notice.' If that doesn't work, 'You can change into your pretty going away outfit now. Don't let it spoil the day.'

When disaster strikes, *e.g.* the cake collapses, take a picture so you can help the bride get compensation as consolation and don't despair, laugh about it afterwards.

THE RECEPTION

At the reception make sure you arrive ahead of the bride to await her arrival and arrange her train. If no usher is available alert a porter to open the door for the bride. If no-one else is available you open doors for the bride.

THE RECEIVING LINE

At very traditional English weddings the bridesmaids do not stand in the receiving line, which is essentially the hosts receiving the guests, thus the mother of the bride, as hostess, her husband, the bride and groom, the groom's parents. When a matron of honour hosts the reception at her house in lieu of the bride's deceased, sick, or absent mother, she heads the line.

Slightly less formal UK and Roman Catholic weddings and American weddings (which are less traditional) often include bridesmaids in the receiving line, but this is not the case at UK Jewish weddings.

WELCOME ROOM

If you are invited to join the line, listen out for introductions so that you know who people are. Shake hands or accept a kiss on the cheek as appropriate, and say a few words – but do not enter long conversations as you will hold up proceedings.

If the receiving line is at the front door, gate or path, and assuming she is not officially part of it, the chief bridesmaid could still stand at the end of the line and point the way to the welcome room, or greet guests entering the welcome room.

At larger formal receptions the toastmaster announces guests approaching the receiving line. Listen for the name and use it when greeting guests coming off the line and directing them to drinks or making introductions. Copy formal titles, 'Your Grace, . . .', though you can lapse into familiarity with friends. Introduce yourself to strangers saying your name distinctly, 'I'm the bride's sister, Anne,' then clearly and enthusiastically introduce the other bridesmaids, especially juniors, 'and this is our youngest sister, Susan'.

Tiny children do not stand in the receiving line because they are not hosts and it would tire them. A bridesmaid might sit at a table where guests sign the visitors' book and direct them to the rail where their clothes are put on a hanger by a younger bridesmaid or pageboy if the reception venue staff cannot do this.

Another bridesmaid could then direct ladies to the bathroom and mirrors. An usher usually takes the men's clothes. Alternatively a bridesmaid keeps each group's coats together, issuing one coat ticket to the head of the family.

A third bridesmaid might point the way to the garden or lounge where drinks are being served, or the marquee.

The ushers may stand singly along a roped path or canopy leading to a marquee, or the ushers and bridesmaids could stand paired as in church.

THE DINING/BANQUETING HALL

The master of ceremonies may announce, 'Ladies and gentlemen, please stand to welcome the bride and groom', and sometimes the wedding march is played, the lights are dimmed and the bride and groom enter, perhaps with spotlights on them, or the lights come on again as they enter. For a theatrical effect common at Greek or Italian weddings the happy couple step through a curtain which draws back on the stage where the band plays and the bride and groom descend an arched stairway, possibly in the same order as the recession, preceded by the pageboy, ring-bearer and flower girl, followed by the bridesmaids. On reaching a flowered arch the bride and groom stop with a ribbon across their path, tied to the sides of the arch.

Or they might enter on a pathway of red carpet between the guests, with bridesmaids and ushers forming an arch of flowers by holding up long-stemmed carnations. The bride and groom walk to the end of the archway where their progress is stopped by a ribbon held by the pageboy and youngest usher. Then the master of ceremonies announces, 'To mark the beginning of your married life together, David and Sandra, will you please untie the ribbon.' The bride and groom pull both ends of the bow in the centre of the ribbon. Or the master of ceremonies asks the groom to cut the ribbon and a member of staff steps forward with a pair of scissors on a tray.

TAKING SEATS AT THE TABLE

The bride and groom walk around the top table, sometimes separately, bride to the right, groom left, guided by the restaurant staff. The bridesmaid does not usually need to hold the bride's train, as this should be done by banquetting staff who see that the bride is seated. Or the bride arrives with the train looped over her (left) arm as she will be holding it later when dancing.

The bride and groom sit down first and only when they are seated do you sit down. You may need to wait for the minister to say grace before you start eating.

The paired pageboy and flower girl could go up to top table to make a presentation to the bride at this point.

BRIDESMAIDS' GIFTS

The bridegroom might hand over wrapped gifts to the bridesmaids privately after the ceremony, and before the guests gather at the receiving line at the reception, or alternatively he might hand over the gifts after or during his speech when he toasts the bridesmaids.

For a theatrical effect the gifts may be presented after the cake-cutting. The band plays a few bars of music, a drum roll or clash of cymbals to get attention, the lights dim or flash on and off, and the restaurant staff wheel in the presents on a trolley, or bring them forward one by one on a circular silver tray, from which the gift is lifted by the bride or groom.

The bride hands the first present to the best man who shakes hands and waits. The groom hands the second present to the chief bridesmaid and kisses her. (The bride also thanks the bridesmaid and kisses her. Sometimes the bride instead of the groom hands the present to the bridesmaid.)

The chief bridesmaid should turn to face the camera while holding onto the present which the donor does not necessarily release. The photographer snaps the bride, groom, best man and bridesmaid with the presents held prominently. The bridesmaid holds her gift at waist level or jointly with the donor.

The best man and chief bridesmaid sit down and other bridesmaids and ushers get ready to stand up and go forward. Another pair follow in the same order as the recession. A gift is handed by the bride to the chief usher, and so on, until lastly the pageboy and flower girl are called. On each occasion a photo is often taken of the two recipients with the bride and groom.

You may be at a loss for words when others have already said what you wanted to say when you are presented with a gift. Some phrases to keep in mind are, 'It is so pretty, suits me ... goes beautifully with the dress. It's just what I've always wanted. How thoughtful of you. I shall treasure it. I can wear it at my ... You're a darling, an angel.' Finally say, 'Thank you!' hug the donor and give her a kiss. If the gift can be worn, put it on. Don't say, 'You shouldn't have spent so much'. You don't want her to regret it and feel badly, do you? Say something complimentary such as, 'That's really generous of you.'

If the donor says, 'I hope you haven't already got one,' don't reveal that you have by saying, 'I have – but it doesn't matter'.

When shown someone else's gift say, 'It's gorgeous ... looks terrific on you ... what a lovely present'.

ARRANGING INTRODUCTIONS

You could ask the bride beforehand to show you a list of the guests and a table plan. Find out which guests have something in common and ask the bride who should meet whom. When making introductions first tell the important person who the less important one is. The order is VIPs such as titled people first, the married before the unmarried, and those senior in position or age before younger ones. Great-aunt is told the name of the five-year old. The woman is the person to whom the man must be introduced, 'Anne, may I introduce Philip.' Then make the introduction the other way round so that both people hear the other's name again. 'Philip, this is Anne'.

Add facts you know about them to get their conversation started, their relationship to the bride or groom, homeland, hobbies, and employment. This gets shy boys talking and saves luckless girls from asking, 'What do you do?' and getting the conversation-stopping reply, 'As little as possible.'

DINNER TABLE SEATING

A traditional top table has the bride and groom in the centre, with their parents either side, each seated with their own spouse at ethnic weddings, the bride's father next to her, his wife by him. The groom has his mother on his other side and her husband beside her. This also suits people from close family backgrounds where husbands and wives are inseparable. When you have just one bridesmaid the top table can seat eight with the best man by the bride's mother and the bridesmaid on the end by the groom's father.

Grandparents or the minister and his wife might be also placed on the top table, with younger bridesmaids and ushers with youngsters on another table.

When bridesmaids and ushers are members of the family the top table is extended to include all six. Two long trestle tables are placed L-shape along two sides of the room, meeting at the corner. The bride and groom sit in the corner, diagonally side by side where the tables meet, with the bride's family, her bridesmaids and parents on her side; the groom's ushers and parents along his table. This suits a room where, for example, one hundred guests are seated at tables of eight or ten, so that there are eight to ten other tables.

To accommodate more pageboys and flower girls in a

smaller room, the top table is extended by two wing tables at right angles.

The top table has members of the wedding party only, no fiancees of bridesmaids nor husbands of matrons of honour.

SMALLER RECEPTIONS

When twenty of the fifty guests are family the numbers on the top table would dominate the room, with only three tables of ten guests. So instead of one top table the family is divided with bridesmaids on the bride's youngsters' table and older relatives on her parents' table.

The bride and groom sit at a top table with their attendants facing into the room. The bridesmaid's bouquets are placed on the table in front of them as decoration. The bride's parents sit with the groom's parents and the minister and his wife, any grandparents, the sisters and brothers of the parents or other older folk.

SUPERVISING CHILDREN

During the ceremony and at the reception buffet or pre-dinner drinks the older bridesmaid stands behind or beside the younger one, talks to her, if necessary takes her to the toilet, reminds her to smile, says 'hush' subtly by holding a finger to her lips or says 'whisper to me'.

Place a napkin on her lap when she is eating or wash her hands so she does not get sticky fingers on her dress. Stop her sitting down on the dirty floor when she gets tired; say, 'come and sit on my lap'. The younger one may go home early before the evening celebrations. At some weddings there is a party bus which parks outside. Children eat inside the decorated coach during speeches, and play games related to weddings. A boy of about 12 can be dressed up as a bride and told to speak with a falsetto voice. A girl is dressed as a groom and prompted to propose, 'Will you marry me?'. The answer is 'not likely'. The prompt suggests, 'Ask "Is she rich?"' which becomes, 'Have you got any money?'

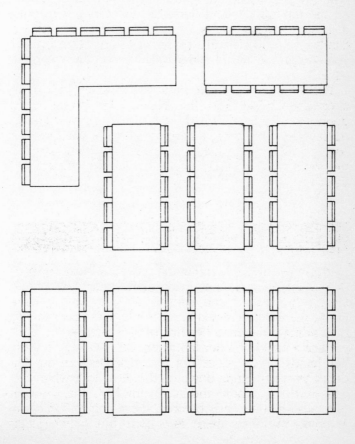

Pass the Parcel can be played as Pass the Ring. Each player takes the ring off the hand of the person on his left, places it on his own finger, and is out if wearing it when the music stops. Prizes are given to all children by the end of the party. Such games can be more fun for children than boring wedding dinners. At large weddings such as Greek or Asian there are sometimes sufficient children to occupy a separate party room.

AFTER THE MEAL

Arrange for the master of ceremonies to allow you time after eating to retire with the bride to her changing room and reapply her lipstick and yours. He announces to guests that you have a five minute break. Help the bride remove a removable train, bodice or bolero for dancing. However, make sure you are present when a minister is called upon to say grace at the end of the meal before smoking is permitted, and of course everyone must return in time to hear speeches, toasts and telegrams.

CUTTING THE CAKE

The most common wedding disaster is the toppling cake. If you see it leaning or the icing cracking summon the banqueting manager. At home if icing on the lower level isn't solid you must dismantle the cake and reassemble it just for the cake cutting. The 'cement' cake which cannot be cut bends or breaks the knife. Stab the cake through the centre to get it started. Cut it and fill the cut with butter icing.

DANCING

The master of ceremonies might call the bride and groom onto the dance floor, then after they have circled the floor once he calls the best man and chief bridesmaid by name, 'Please welcome Peter and Belinda'. The audience applauds as they walk onto the dance floor. After a few moments' dancing the other bridesmaids and ushers are called in pairs, often after the bride's parents, and the groom's parents, until the top table is empty. The photographer photographs the bride dancing and bridesmaids dancing with ushers.

The chief bridesmaid or bride might hint that ushers invite the younger bridesmaids and single ladies lacking partners to dance. Bridesmaids could dance with each other but it is better to provide partners.

DISTRIBUTING SUGARED ALMOND FAVOURS

You may be asked to distribute cake and favours such as bonbonnieres (sugared almonds in coloured lace) unless the bride wants to take the favours. Keep extras for later arrivals, particularly children, so no-one feels neglected. If there are insufficient favours handy don't keep a disappointed child waiting: donate your own and seek a replacement.

CATCHING THE BOUQUET

When the bride throws the bouquet she symbolizes the marital status passing from the bride to whoever catches the bouquet. The bride may throw her bouquet from the top of the stairs to the bridesmaids below. When there are no stairs she can throw the bouquet over her shoulder on the dance floor to the bridesmaids lined up behind her. If there is only one bridesmaid the master of ceremonies calls all the single women for this event.

Who should catch it? In theory there is a contest. In practice it should be a girl eligible to marry. However, a good-natured older bridesmaid who sets no store by such superstition might let her younger sister catch it, or catch it and hand it to her.

The bouquet is not always thrown. The bride may wish to keep it or give it to a sick relative or charity. A florist collecting the bouquet to preserve it for the bride can supply an identical bouquet for throwing.

THROWING THE GARTER

The bride's garter is usually thrown to the ushers or to the single men. Alternatively throwing the garter to the girls supposedly transfers some of the bride's sexual power to the bridesmaid who captures it. Putting your piece of cake under your pillow is also supposed to inspire you to dream of a future husband.

THE COUPLE'S DEPARTURE

The chief bridesmaid helps the bride change. When the bride and groom are both dressed ready to leave, call the bride's parents for a private hug, goodwill message and farewell kiss. Remind the bride to say goodbye privately to her in-laws too. Check that the hire car or vehicle has arrived and is decorated (ask the best man or second bridesmaid to tell you) before letting the bridal couple exit.

The photographer may want to snap the bride and groom getting into the car alone, without crowds of arms and legs obscuring it, then a picture of bride and groom leaving in it with guests throwing rice.

Checklist – At The Reception

Sit at the top table or a table near the bride.

If required assist with catering.

Catch the bouquet.

Help the bride change into her going away outfit.

Return the bride's dress.

Reception location: Name, address, phone ....
    date .... time ....

Bandleader's Name ....

Master of Ceremonies' name ....

Banqueting manager's name ....

Names of VIP relatives ....

Names of VIP guests ....

Guest departure time ....

DECORATING THE CAR

Hire cars arrive decorated with a white ribbon. A borrowed car must be cleaned. Cover seats with white sheets to protect dresses. Decorate a red car with white ribbon, and a white car with white plus perhaps a colour such as pink to match dresses. Place flowers on the back shelf. The car colour should not clash with bridesmaids' dresses.

The bridesmaids may be asked to help ushers decorate the going away car using flowers and ribbons. Flowers on wire from bouquets can create artistic effects. Balloons decorating the hall can be re-used to decorate the car. A Just Married sign looks neater when made in advance. Write messages or the first names of the couple with shaving cream (messy but easily removed) or lipstick (hard to remove). Confetti can be sprinkled in the car or on the back parcel shelf. A music cassette might be supplied for a long journey.

Thoughtless ushers sometimes plan silly tricks. The bridesmaid who suspects that this may happen should ensure no harm is done. While the chief bridesmaid helps the bride change another bridesmaid could 'help' the groomsmen with decoration and say, 'That's enough!' if things get out of hand. She might bring a neatly written card and discuss early on with the groomsmen how to attach it, so establishing their plans.

What is excessive? I saw a car completely covered with white shaving foam so it was impossible to drive. Don't obscure windows or otherwise delay the getaway, especially if the bride and groom have to catch a plane.

A simple countryside pony and trap can be kitted out prettily with white reins and white roses in the lamps.

Tin cans are often tied on the back of the car. A more elegant musical effect is obtained by attaching jingle bells. Ring cowbells and handbells, bang gongs and clack castanets, or you could even serenade the couple with ethnic music using guitars and accordians as they drive off!

Stationers sell balloons with the words Just Married. Helium-filled balloons with the same wording are sold by balloon specialists. Guests might throw confetti, rose petals, or rice after the car.

Checklist – Decorating the Car

Decorating the Car

Umbrellas supplied by .... colour ....

   ribbons supplied by .... colour ....

Balloons .... colour ....

Flowers for parcel shelf ....

   flower on internal mirror support?

   ribbons on left and right internal doorpost straps?

Do confer with the best man and ushers about decorations

Do make decorations pretty not messy (finger messages in foam look untidy on a smart car)

Do make conventional Just Married sign in advance

Do plan who will hide it

Do plan an extra personalised slogan or pretty surprise

Do rehearse the decorating once – perhaps on the best man's car – to check how long it takes

Do check how the decorations can be safely removed and supply any required cloth in the glovebox

Do clear front windows by using the windscreen wipers

Don't obscure windows

Don't let balloons fall inside the pedal area

Don't make the car undrivable

Do advise bride and groom to threaten to daub pranksters' cars Not Married

Don't use lipsticks or other items which might stain clothes and damage cars

Don't forget a pre-arranged signal so the decorators

know when they can start in secret

Don't forget a pre-arranged signal to tell whoever is helping the bride change that they have finished

Don't forget your camera to photograph the going away car

HIRED CARS

Don't expect to decorate a hired car

Do check if the going away car is hired (the chauffeur won't allow daubing)

Do check whether the hired car company can supply a Just Married sign and ask what else they can supply

Do check on the internal flower decorations. Add your posy if the hire car decorations are not sufficient.

AFTER THE RECEPTION PARTY

You may be asked to distribute flowers from tables to the hosts or guests according to the bride's wishes. Clear up the catering, helping the bride's mother pack and carry the cake tier she's saving.

You can store bouquets wrapped in the fridge as instructed until the florist collects, or next day deliver bouquets to be pressed. As the bride will be away now, take her and your dresses to the cleaners as soon as possible before stains have time to set. Return hired clothes to the shop or send the bride's dress to her home if she left in going away clothes. Professional cleaning and packing services are offered for dresses.

You may be able to help by attaching cards to cake boxes sent to guests unable to attend. Send wedding announcements and photos of the bride and groom to friends abroad who were not invited.

Some bridesmaids who are close friends, acknowledge safe arrival of presents explaining that the bride will shortly reply personally after her honeymoon.

NEWSPAPER ANNOUNCEMENTS

Order the newspapers which will carry the wedding announcements and save them for yourself and other members of the family. The newspaper announcement will include something like 'The bride was attended by Miss Anne Pink and Susan Blue.' Bridesmaids over the age of 16 are described as Miss. You don't need to say Miss for a girl under 16 because she cannot be legally married. Each of the bridesmaids will want an original copy of the announcement so phone the others to tell them the newspaper is out or buy enough copies for everyone.

WHILE THEY'RE AWAY

Department stores can be instructed not to send gifts while the bride and groom are away on honeymoon. Printed cards are impersonal as the sole acknowledgement of a gift. However, the bridesmaid can add a handwritten line that the bride will be writing in person on her return.

While the bride and groom are away put leftover food from the wedding reception in their freezer. If you live near their new home, move letters, parcels, newspapers, dustbins and telltale signs that the house is empty to prevent burglary. Water new plants. Write a note of what has been done, reminders of calls to be returned, and a welcome home message. Leave fresh flowers, fruit, bread, biscuits, milk, coffee and wine or arrange a welcome home party.

HONEYMOON NIGHT AT HOME

In the old days the bridesmaids would help the bride prepare for bed, help her remove the wedding gown, hang up her clothes, prepare a scented bath or bowl of hot water, let down her hair and comb it out, help her put on her nightdress and turn down the bed for her.

If the couple are spending their first night at home near the reception you can send one of the bridesmaids to decorate the bedroom after the bride has left for the wedding, perhaps during the evening dancing, as a surprise. The Greeks and Romans used red satin sheets. The Chinese hung red paper over the bed. You need to keep the items for decoration somewhere handy, watch the time, and make sure the girls doing the decorating have transport and a spare door key.

For a happy 'your family loves you' effect, have a new welcome mat or a banner in the hall visible as they open the front door saying, 'Welcome to your new Home', or 'Hello Mr and Mrs Montagu', and in the bedroom balloons from the reception and a congratulations card.

Make the home like a luxurious, romantic hotel honeymoon suite with fresh flowers, fresh fruit by the bed, a small tin of biscuits, a bottle of mineral water and glasses on a tray, fresh perfumed soap and toiletries in the bathroom, embroidered his and hers towels, curtains drawn, bedsheets turned down on both sides with a flower as decoration or a chocolate, bedside lights switched on and mood music playing.

For fun you could have jokey pillows saying YES on one side and NO on the other turned to the YES side. Pink and blue crackers could be saved from the reception (one of each) with a small gift for him in the blue cracker, a small gift for her in the pink cracker. Wedding dolls could be placed on the bed, or teddy bears in bride and groom outfits. Overnight place signs outside on the gate and garden wall and against the front door saying, 'JUST MARRIED. DO NOT DISTURB'. If you are living or staying in the same house and rise earlier it would make a lovely surprise to place a tray with croissants and orange juice on a table outside the door with a note.

ANNIVERSARIES

The bride may invite her former bridesmaids to a Christening or the anniversary party when the upper tier of the wedding cake is served. If you are invited, take along the wedding photographs. Some couples simply have wedding anniversary cards and a quiet candle-lit dinner for two. Remember to send a card.

If the bride isn't planning a party you could invite the bridal couple to dinner at an unspecified restaurant but drive them to your home where the bridesmaids are wearing bridesmaids' dresses for a surprise anniversary party! For a party at home buy from stationers balloons with the words Happy Anniversary. Play The Anniversary Waltz. The groom buys the bride major presents such as diamonds for the diamond wedding anniversary. Other guests buy smaller gifts, trinkets and cards reflecting the theme. If you want to buy a party gift here are the traditional anniversaries and their modern alternatives.

1 paper or clocks
2 cotton or china
3 leather, crystal or glass
4 fruit, flowers, books or appliances
5 wood or silverware
6 sugar, candy, iron or wood
7 wooden, copper, wool or desk sets
8 bronze, pottery, linens or lace
9 willow pattern, pottery or leather
10 tin, aluminium or diamond jewellery
11 steel or fashion jewellery
12 silk, linen or pearls
13 lace, textiles or furs
14 ivory or gold jewellery
15 crystal or watches
20 china or platinum
25 silver
30 pearl or diamond

35 coral or jade
40 ruby
45 sapphire
50 gold
55 emerald
60/70/75 diamonds

Complete wedding checklist

Complete Wedding Checklist
Bride's name, home address and phone ....
Rendez-vous date .... time ....
Bride's parents' names, home address and phone ....
Groom's name, home address and phone ....
Groom's parents' names, address and phone
numbers ....
Children's names ....
Nanny/au pair/childminder's/babysitter's name ....
Bride's grandparents' names ....
Groom's grandparents' names ....
Best Man's name, home address and phone ....
Matron of Honour's name address and phone ....
Chief bridesmaid's name address and phone ....
Clothes supplier's names address and and phone ....
Delivery date and time ....
Hairdresser's name address and phone ....
Apointment date and time .... Assistant ....
Taxi company name, address and phone ....
Arrival date and time ....
Doctor's name, address and phone ....
Dentist's name address and phone ....
Minister's name, address and phone ....
Minister's wife's name ....
Bandleader's name ....
Master of Ceremonies' name ....
Banqueting manager's name ....
Names of VIP relatives ....
Names of VIP guests ....

Engagement party location: Name, address, phone ....
contact .... date .... time ....
Hen party location: Name, address, phone ....
date .... time ....
Stag party/Bachelor dinner location:
Name, address, phone ....
date .... time ....
Shower party host's name, address and phone ....
date ....time ....
Out of town guest's party:
Host's name, address and phone ....
date .... time ....
Rehearsal party location:
Name, address, phone ....
date .... time ....
Department store with wedding list:
Name, address, phone ....
Wedding ceremony location name,
address, phone ....
date .... time ....
Reception location:
Name, address, phone ....
date .... time ....
Honeymoon location:
Name, address, phone ....
Travel agent name address, phone ....
Airline name, address, reservations phone number ....
Airport's airline flight departure/arrival enquiry
    number ....
Hotel name, address, phone number, fax number ....
Railway station address, phone ....
Bridesmaids return train/flight/taxi from:
Location address and phone ....
date .... time ....
Newspaper name, address, phone ....
Official photographer's name, address, phone ....
Film printing and developing company name, address,

phone ....
Bride and groom's return from honeymoon:
date .... time .... tour operator ....
airport .... airline .... flight number ....
Flight arrivals information phone number: ....
Airport taxi phone number: ....
Train station ....
Bride and groom's new name, address and phone ....
Dog kennel/petminder's name, address and phone ....
Collection date and time ....

BUDGET WEDDINGS

The chief bridesmaid is likely to be much more involved in the practicalities of the day at a budget wedding and she can help in many ways from cooking to helping serve the drinks.

DRESSES

When budgets are tight, you can make your own dresses or have them made by your mother, the bride's mother or a seamstress. Pattern books can be obtained from libraries. Second hand dresses can sometimes be bought from the shops or from individuals through advertisements in local newspapers.

If you plan to use a white or pastel dress, blouse or jumper you can decorate the neckline, sleeves or cuffs with ribbon roses bought from department store sewing sections. The same ribbon roses can be sewn onto a handbag or purse made from material cut off the dress hem, or attached to an Alice band or hair ribbon, and sewn or pinned to your shoes. You could also try to find period dresses and shawls, evening bags, buttons and beads at jumble sales, markets, or by asking older relatives.

PLANNING FOOD

List the number of guests and calculate how many the house and garden or nearby hall accommodate and decide whether to entertain everyone together, or older relatives to a sit-down lunch and younger people to an evening buffet party and disco.

After tasting samples of fruit cakes at bakeries or bridal shows, if you think you can make a better cake, you could still have your home-made cake decorated by a bakery. A cake covered with marzipan, plain white icing and a simple border can supplement pieces distributed from the bottom layer of the elaborate cake. If the bride and groom or guests do not all like heavy fruit cake, the top layer of the cake can be sponge, the bottom layer fruit cake.

Make a test cake in advance. Recipes for wedding cakes are available from bridal magazines, women's magazines, manufacturers of cake ingredients, sugar, icing sugar, flour and dried fruit, and suppliers of icing, marzipan and decoration kits. Visit kitchen shops which supply sets of cake tins in different sizes, solid white or transparent columns, and bride and groom cake decorations. Other symbols include bells, horseshoes or miniature silver car numberplates with the letters of the bride's and groom's names.

Library books on catering for large numbers can be supplemented by asking home economics teachers at the bridesmaids' schools for buffet recipes and advice. Bridemaids may need to loan space in their fridges and transport food at the last moment.

SIMPLE FOOD

To minimize cooking and preparation on the day prepare cold foods such as quiches and meringues in advance. A simple menu is melon, then cold meats, fresh or smoked fish, cheeses, an easy to prepare filling savoury like smoked salmon and cream cheese on bagels, or sandwiches made from pre-cut loaves sliced horizontally. The simplest dessert is strawberries and cream. Have net covers or a supply of plastic film to keep off insects.

If the weather is unpredictable and might be chilly, plan an easily prepared hot dish such as soup. For a hot day have a good supply of ice for drinks or as a bed to keep trays of food cool. Slices of fruit can be arranged prettily in fans and circles on ice, but it is worth planning an elaborate centrepiece of either food or flowers. If you run out of food for guests who stay on all evening phone for pizzas to be delivered, one vegetarian, another meat.

You could also make your own wedding favours for each guest. Wrap five sugared almonds in a piece of white net tied with a piece of white ribbon.

DRINK

Prepare a tray of drinks, jugs of cold juice, decorated with slices of lemon, a whole strawberry with a cut half way across, balanced on the side of the glass, or sprig of mint, and red or other coloured straws.

Make mint tea from mint tea bags. Or use ordinary tea bags plus chopped mint which you remove using a tea strainer before serving. Place washed fresh mint from your garden in each glass. Serve hot or cold as iced tea.

Champagne cocktail is cheaper than neat champagne or you could use sparking wines. For a pink party have lots of rose wines or pink champagne.

Find out if you can get reductions by buying wine by the case. If not you can please and amuse your guests by having a greater variety of drink than you would have at a banquet where only one type of table wine was allocated. Stock spirits and beers, both light and dark, if your guests require these.

BEFOREHAND

What does the house look like when people arrive? Perhaps you could help out by cleaning the windows and windowsills, mowing the lawn, or steam-clean the carpets, curtains and upholstery (borrowing a machine from a hire shop or relatives) and wash the net curtains. Ushers or children can vacuum carpets, water plants and cut off dead leaves, empty wastebins and do the dusting.

Check the numbers of guests who have replied and count the chairs, tables, crockery, cutlery and glasses available at the house that is to hold the reception. Arrange for extras required to be bought or borrowed and decide who will transport bulky items such as chairs. Try out the table for the wedding cake and the tablecloth. Leave room for the bride and groom to stand behind to cut the cake. If using a small rickety card-table, make sure it is not going to collapse.

PREPARATION FOR THE DAY

Non-cooks can make fruit salad and sandwiches, or stick sausages and cubes of cheese on cocktail sticks. Ask the other bridesmaids and their mothers to hunt through their kitchens for gadgets which cut tomatoes and fruit into fancy shapes. Ask friends who have worked in a bar, restaurant or hotel to demonstrate fancy or fast ways of preparing food. Call the ushers and delegate them to collect wines and glasses from the wineshop. For champagne the tall glass flute with narrow brim is more correct because you lose the bubbles from wide brim glasses. Make a punch, lay out bottles and glasses in groups of triangular or diamond patterns, locate bottle openers and move furniture.

One of the bridesmaids can take the small pageboy or flower girl out of the way for the morning to a park or take them to a video hire shop and then sit with the children while they watch a video. Someone who hates cooking but likes cleaning can tidy the cloakroom, clean the toilets and basins, buy and put out fresh soap, and install full toilet rolls. Clear the hall cupboard or have the best bedroom tidied ready for guests to lay their coats on the beds. Get the ushers and children to make a sign saying 'coats'. The ushers can cut a large piece of white card and draw pencil lines. The children can draw round alphabet letters and colour them in. To guide younger children colour the letter outlines with a broad line first.

DECORATION

Alternatively keep children usefully occupied with an uncle or friend who blows up balloons while others tie balloons onto strings and ribbons. Children can help decide where to attach balloons and fix them on in the agreed designated places. For a unified effect choose a colour theme co-ordinating the surroundings, the tableware, and the bridesmaids' dresses. If the bride's family has insufficient flowers for decorating the tables and your garden is full of blossoms, take some with you.

LAYING TABLES

Keep a list of things to do on the larder or kitchen cupboard or kitchen door. Establish what help is available, if any, for preparing, serving and clearing up. When laying tables never place your fingers inside the wineglass: hold it by the stem; and never place your fingers inside a soup or cereal plate: use the handles or place your hands under the bowl. For a grand effect which costs nothing place saucers or plates under bowls.

ON THE DAY

SERVING FOOD

Stationers sell paper plates which save on washing up and matching partyware such as paper cups and streamers. The bride can economize by having home-made food served by hired staff, or professionally made food which you lay out on a buffet and let guests help themselves. Handing around plates of food is a good way to meet all the guests and gives you a conversation opener.

ENTERTAINMENT

If the groom is to serenade the bride on a guitar, take your photos afterwards, not while he is singing. Perhaps you and the best man can organize and lead a sing-song. You could borrow songbooks from libraries. Practice the songs until you know them by heart. Write out or duplicate the words on paper sheets for guests.

SERVING FOOD AND DRINKS

After cake-cutting carry plates with pieces of cake to the guests. If you are not giving each guest a plate take a pile of paper serviettes. Before serving tea and coffee, place sugar and milk on each table. Offer second cups of tea before spiriting away the crockery. Collect dirty cups and saucers afterwards to minimize accidents and make the place look tidy.

If you all have time and live nearby do some cleaning up after the party or return next day. Another way to relieve the burden on the bride's mother is to organize professional cleaning up. Call a housecleaning service or find out whether your own family's help (if you have one) is willing to clean elsewhere if you arrange the transport for them.

BUDGETING HINTS

List your own budget hints to help the bride. For example sales at jewellery shops sometimes have a catalogue of items which can be posted – or even sent abroad. Home-made gifts can include cushions, curtains and bookends.

WEDDINGS AROUND THE WORLD

Weddings have different customs and styles around the world, for of course they reflect the culture of the land they are held in. For example in Spain, Italy and Yugoslavia a child carries the ring instead of the best man. There are countless other variations and this chapter will introduce you to some of them.

To get ideas for making the wedding different go with the bride to a Wedding Fayre. Many are held in large cities, particularly in autumn and spring, usually in big hotels where local companies set up stands representing bridal wear shops, cake and wine suppliers, photographers, video companies and car hire firms. Advertisements in the back of the local newspapers may also give you ideas, such as hiring traditional characters dressed as chimney sweeps for weddings.

Before participating in a wedding, especially one involving unfamiliar ceremonies, it helps to see a video of a similar wedding. This can be done at bridal show, by visiting the office or home of the video film company director, or by asking the bride's friends, acquaintances from work, and school. They will be delighted to show you a film of a family wedding and explain the customs. For ethnic weddings where one side is of a different nationality, and for weddings with guests such as Hindus and Sikhs, an introduction to or reminder of their rituals is useful. The bride needs to see videos to decide which parts of her wedding and which people should be filmed. Bridesmaids and other female attendants can see which styles of dress are prettiest, which duties they must perform and how to behave confidently and elegantly.

TRANSLATING

At the reception the master of ceremonies is usually someone who can make announcements in two languages. If you are bilingual or have a smattering of another language you could look up a few everyday words in the dictionary and keep a note of them in your bag to help with translating. It helps to know the dozen or so most relevant words.

For practical reasons and as a courtesy to the bride and the minister or officiant, find out about the traditions of the church or religious establishment you will attend. Use the phone directory. Look up Religious Organisations to find the head office and Places of Worship to locate the individual church/ministers and their views. Find out about how to address the minister, the specific ritual of the marriage ceremony such as candle-lighting, the customs at the reception meal, and daily observances such as diet. The following notes on practices will guide you about which points to check.

RELIGIONS

BAPTIST

The Baptist ceremony can be similar to that in an

Anglican church and Anglicans might get married in a Baptist church. Baptists are members of the free church and ministers have freedom to make their own decisions about who they will marry. The minister will be referred to as Reverend John Smith or whatever. Veils and so on are at the discretion of the bride. Brides and bridesmaids therefore have plenty of freedom and frequently choose to follow the fashions currently set by royalty.

QUAKER

Send non-Quaker guests a leaflet about the Quaker ceremony in advance so they are prepared for periods of silent contemplation. Bridesmaids sit beside the couple. Alcohol is not usually served in Meeting House premises, but both ceremony and reception could be held at a home. If the bride is not wearing a white gown but a day dress, the bridesmaids should not be more formally nor more elaborately dressed than the bride.

JEHOVAH'S WITNESSES

A member of the bride's family who is not a Jehovah's Witness may be the bridesmaid. Bridesmaids may follow or precede the bride in the procession. The bride and groom are married by an elder. The veil is optional, and bridesmaids follow the bride in the recession. No confetti is thrown because this practice is based on a pagan custom.

IRISH/CATHOLIC

Divorce is not currently (1990) freely available in Eire. Therefore if the groom has married before and been divorced abroad the bride and bridesmaid may have to travel abroad for a church wedding – or a register office wedding. Certain divorces granted by the church will not be recognised by the state and vice versa. Laws on contraception also differ from Britain. Therefore if the bride faces problems or confusion the bridesmaid may be called upon to give advice or moral support.

JEWISH

Jewish marriages usually take place in a synagogue in England, not at home. During the ceremony the bridesmaid waits at the foot of the bimah (dais). A copy of the marriage service with preface and commentary by the Chief Rabbi is available in advance. Among other observations he points out that Judaism is rational and the groom's breaking the glass underfoot is symbolic but not 'lucky' as Judaism knows no superstitions.

The bride is not supposed to wear jewellery, apart from the ring, so it would be inappropriate for the bridesmaids to wear a lot of jewellery. Customs vary from the most orthodox where men and women sit separately in synagogue, through the Reform to the Liberal. Ultra-orthodox men and women do not dance together nor shake hands.

Bridesmaids are not in the receiving line, and at the reception at orthodox weddings women do not serve the wine so you wait for the men at your table or the banqueting staff to pour. The meal will probably be strictly kosher. The only mistake you can make is asking for milk or cream or ice cream or cheese at dessert because milk and meat are not mixed. After a meat meal no milk is served for some hours so the cake cutting is delayed until after the meal when tea can be served with milk. There will be kosher wine and even kosher sugared almond favours. See that the pageboy has his head covered by wearing his skullcap when the rabbi is ready to begin the long grace after the meal.

UK JEWISH ORTHODOX CEREMONY

Order a synagogue wedding canopy (chuppah) embroidered with bride's and groom's names in Hebrew and English; check canopy colour; order flowers for canopy pillars. The pageboy or ringbearer will be wearing a skullcap as headcovering like the ushers, e.g. in white or black or red or blue velvet. Orthodox Jewish women and bride sit on the right. At the end of the orthodox ceremony nuts and rice are thrown over the couple 'be fruitful and multiply'.

The Jewish reception: provide the rabbi with wine, bread and salt for the blessing; provide paper skullcaps for men to wear during grace. The rabbi makes the loyal toast to The Queen after the main course, then a toast to The President of the state of Israel. Dancing may take place during the meal. The rabbi makes the long blessing (grace) after dinner. Orthodox groups wait at least two hours after meat before serving milk, therefore if coffee and tea are to accompany cake-cutting it takes place later.

MUSLIM

The bride must have a married attendant, who is a relative or intimate friend to advise about the wedding night. She can choose a second attendant who might be unmarried, but both attendants – never more than two – are members of her family. The attendant helps decorate the bride's hands, on the palms as on any festive occasion, but also on the backs because it is a wedding, and the bride's feet, which are seen because one enters a mosque barefoot (though women can wear popsox). The attendant's hands are decorated less elaborately than the bride's and her feet are not decorated. The bride wears white, the bridesmaid a contrasting colour. Two attendants would usually be dressed alike.

HINDU

Hindu ceremonies do not require bridesmaids. The bride, wearing red or pink, might sit under a canopy on the stage at a town hall, with as many as 1500 guests. Hindu guests at your reception might require vegetarian food.

BUDDHIST

The Buddhist couple might go to a temple or monastery (vihara) to be blessed by the monks in front of a statue of Buddha and the chanting of blessing might be done by family members including the parents or brothers and sisters. No alcohol is served at the reception. Traditions vary from country to country, and a wedding date considered auspicious for the couple might be chosen.

EUROPE

FRANCE

In France the maid of honour and other bridesmaids are all called demoiselle d'honneur (damsel of honour). The best man is a garcon d'honneur (boy of honour), not to be confused with the pageboy. The witness is called a temoin. There may be two pyramid-shape profiterole cakes, one in front of the bride, one in front of the groom. The wedding disco often lasts until the early hours. Attendants jubilantly invade the newlyweds' bedroom next morning to photograph them wearing amusing pyjama outfits.

At a French Jewish wedding at synagogue (which must be preceded by a civil wedding ceremony), the flower girl may go around the reception with her basket collecting money, just small coins.

ITALY

Four or five bridesmaids escort the bride shopping or sightseeing to protect her from the attentions of passing Romeos. At the reception the cake has fountains and arches, for example three tiers plus arches to four surrounding cakes.

SPAIN

Bridesmaids are usually small children. Orange blossom is sewn onto the bride's attire for good luck, usually in petticoats, and wedding dresses have blossom sewn on the centre of the back hem. A white fan may be carried by the bride. Rice is thrown, as in Italy, and bonbonnieres are given.

HOLLAND

In the Netherlands the 'bridesmaid' could be the bride's grandmother.

SCANDINAVIA

In Finland there is usually only one attendant to the bride, no small bridesmaids and pageboys.

GERMANY

The bride 'braut' usually has a young bridesmaid 'brautjungfer'. Society weddings copying the English style might include multiple attendants and a pageboy, 'pagenjunge'.

GREECE

A Greek Orthodox ceremony is spoken and changed in Greek. The religious father is called the papas. Several attendants called best women pay the bride a sum of money and are obliged to choose the bride as their best women at their marriages, when they will receive the equivalent gift. Smaller girls carry tall candles about four foot high on lace bases, one standing either side of the altar.

The brides attendants' dresses co-ordinate with the bride's, and during the reception money or envelopes containing money will be pinned onto the bride's dress. The toast is yamas *i.e.* to us, and iyea sas, to you. Champagne or sparkling wine will probably appear before retsina, wine and beer which will be available later in the evening. Practice the steps of Greek dancing, (to tunes such as those from Zorba the Greek) which is done in lines of single sex or mixed sex groups.

On a Greek island where restaurants are not big enough to accommodate all the guests they might occupy three restaurants alongside each other or around a central square. Bride's attendants accompany the bride or separate to visit all the restaurants. Before visiting Greece learn some of the Greek alphabet, so you can read signposts and maps to get the bridesmaids safely back to your hotel.

USSR

The USSR is officially athiest but Soviet people in other parts of the world celebrate Christian, Jewish or Muslim weddings and have ceremonies reflecting different regions and ethnic groups *e.g.* Ukrainian. The bridal couple might enter the wedding reception through an arch, fresh flower arches and helium-filled balloons could be behind the tables, and the elaborate cake might have fountains. Vodka and whisky would be on the table, and the meal might extend over two and a half hours with everybody dancing between courses.

AMERICA

SURPRISE PARTIES

The surprise party is popular. The bridesmaid either assists the bride in surprising the groom, or assists the other bridesmaids and ushers in preparing a surprise party for both bride and groom. The bride and groom or both might be told to arrive at a friend's house ready to proceed to a restaurant. At the house they find banners and friends and relatives who have gathered, some flying in from faraway places, distant cities and states, even from overseas, to enjoy the party.

The chief bridesmaid who keeps a note of the names, addresses and phone numbers of wedding guests can also organise a surprize first anniversary party with the same guests. Do not tell children in case they accidentally give away the secret. Party shops and greetings cards shops sell banners and balloons saying Congratulations and other suitable goods.

Americans sometimes employ a wedding organizer, a paid professional so the chief bridesmaid has less to do with planning the wedding reception. However, Americans organize more pre-wedding entertaining in which the bridesmaids are usually involved.

BRIDAL SHOWERS

American bridal showers are parties attended only by women at which the bride is given a shower of small gifts, and are held about one month before the wedding.

Parties are not held in the bride's home or hosted by a sister or immediate family as this looks like touting for gifts. Presents are not sent in advance but brought in person and opened by the bride in front of all the guests for general amusement.

More than one shower may be held, as they may be organized by different groups such as colleagues from work, family, neighbours, the local club, old school-friends, neighbours, sports or social club, or even the bridesmaids!

GROUP HOSPITALITY

The hotel might arrange a hospitality suite for a group of foreign guests, *e.g.* 15 English people visiting an American city to attend the wedding of an English bride marrying an American. The hospitality suite would contain an all-day buffet or one set up whenever the group returned to the hotel.

THE BRIDESMAIDS' LUNCH

The bride-to-be holds the bridesmaids' lunch about a fortnight or a week before the wedding. She invites the bridesmaids, their spouses and fiances, and parents of younger children. The bride's cake, a heart or bell-shaped sponge party cake can decorate the table (the groom's cake being the traditional heavy fruit cake). Gifts to bridesmaids might be presented on each place setting, marked with placecard, gift tag. Place settings are in the same colour scheme as the wedding. Alternatively gifts to bridesmaids may be presented at the rehearsal dinner.

The bridesmaids might present in return a guestbook and a ring pillow, or select from the gift registry, the bride's wedding present list at a nearby store. In America it is customary for attendants to pay for their own clothes.

THE REHEARSAL DINNER

The Friday night rehearsal dinner hosted by the groom's parents might be more formal than the wedding itself. Everybody might be given nametags, which the bridesmaids would assist in typing or writing neatly in advance. Speeches are made by the bride and groom, by all bridesmaids on receiving their gifts, and by all the guests.

THE WEDDING

The buttonhole *i.e.* flowers for the buttonhole (UK) is the boutonniere (USA). Bridesmaids might wear a mid-calf dress which the Americans call a 'tea length dress', and if there are numerous bridesmaids a changing room is provided. See that it is equipped with an iron and ironing board, hairdrier, curling tongs, sewing kit, hand mirror and full length mirror. The bride might pay for the hairdresser.

Visit the hairdresser before your old hairstyle has fallen out completely, or have a photograph showing yourself in your usual style or take a magazine picture of the style you want. Hair grips (UK) are called Bobby pins (USA).

You might have a perm before leaving home even if you expect to get your hair done abroad on the wedding day. You need dual voltage hair-driers and curling tongs and adapters to use them in both the UK and USA. When travelling others in your group might appreciate borrowing yours.

In the procession the ushers/groomsmen may precede the bridesmaids or be paired up with them. The top table (UK) is the head table (USA), cutlery is called flatware, the wedding ring is the wedding band, and the person marrying the bride and groom is the officiant.

AMERICAN JEWISH

Be prepared to say or hear some of the following: 'I wish you long life,' a thoughtful wish especially to someone who has had sickness or bereavement; 'I wish you well to wear it,' to someone who has bought or been given new clothes or received a gift of jewellery; and 'Please God by you,' *i.e.* may you be the next to have the good fortune, in the wedding context meaning to be a bride. Mazel tov (literally good star) means good luck or congratulations.

The orthodox Jewish groom arranges the bride's veil in the bride's dressing room before the ceremony. The more orthodox synagogues require ladies to have their heads covered.

WITNESS

A witness to the ketuba (Jewish marriage contract stating the groom's responsibility for maintenance in the event of divorce or his death) cannot be a close relative of the bride or groom, an extension of the old ruling in Deuteronomy 24.16, that a son cannot bear witness against his father.

The Jewish maid of honour holds the marriage document (ketubah) which the bride is given before she states her consent, lifts the veil so the bride can drink wine, lifts the bride's veil again for the bride to sip the second cup of wine, and readjusts the veil, or removes it entirely if it is attached by pins.

Useful books as gifts to the bridal couple can be bought in USA bookshops or Jewish museums and can be used by you as reference.

ASIAN AND ORIENTAL

In Hong Kong passing tourists are likely to want to photograph an oriental bride wearing the usual white dress, and probably the groom, too. In such cases, and during formal photographs, the bridesmaid should stand guard over the gifts. She may be called by the bride to join in the photographs.

For a Chinese style wedding the bride can wear a red dress made of silk and gold thread embroidery with beads of gold metal or plastic, her hair up in a bun secured by a long pin, decorated with jewellery. She might have three bridesmaids, one older, a second one younger, probably the same age as the bride, under 21, a teenager, and a flower girl distributing paper petals. An older bride such as a widow remarrying might wear a cheong sum (long tight dress split both sides) in lucky red.

Bridesmaids might wear pink. On mainland China, instead of the white wedding cake more usual in Hong Kong, you might have a steamed red cake, eaten hot or cold, containing small red beans. On mainland China and Hong Kong you would lift your bowl up towards your mouth when eating, but this is not done in Japan.

Chinese style weddings in Hong Kong or Singapore may have the equivalent of bridesmaids 'sisters for the day' at the brides house. They demand money from the groom before letting him collect the bride. He pretends to bargain but has the anticipated amount of money prepared in a red envelope. Number nine is lucky while four is unlucky in Mandarin and Cantonese. Avoid the number 14 which sounds like 'sure to die' when you say it, but 13 is lucky beçause it sounds like 'sure to live'.

JAPAN

The traditional Japanese bride wears a white kimono, white obi (sash), a pyramid shaped hat and white face make-up to co-ordinate with her outfit. She might change into a white wedding dress then one or two cocktail dresses of any colour such as white, pink or red. She has no bridesmaids but her schoolfriends will sing the school graduation song which translates roughly as 'We will stay friends forever'.

Bow when introduced to a Japanese person, extra low for someone older or of higher status such as the groom's elderly grandmother, or the bride's boss. Introduce people to others of the same rank such as the bride's boss to the groom's boss. A Japanese wedding reception involves many speeches, including the bride's teacher saying what a good pupil she was, and her employer likewise praising her. A video is often taken of the entire reception, not just the highlights.

AUSTRALIA

The person marrying the bride and groom is called the celebrant in Australia. If the bride is an Australian who has met an Englishman while living in England it is popular for them to marry in England and then go to Australia for the honeymoon, or vice versa, perhaps accompanied by the bride's sister or best friend.

The marriage ceremony need not take place in a church or office building but can take place anywhere, indoors or outdoors, in the park or on the beach, in a swimming pool – even parachuting, taking the vows in mid-air with a minister who is also willing to parachute! You can have a barbecue on the beach in Australia at Christmas.

In the capital, Canberra, dominated by embassies, you might expect formality. But in the tropical barrier reef area it is extremely hot in the Australian summer, and people wear lighter looser clothes, suits and ties being oppressive, likewise tights.

For everyday wear in Australia you can buy peaked caps in cotton with material covering the back of the neck. Tropical rainstorms mean the bride in her long train has to have her white skirt and train held up out of the puddles as she emerges from her car or carriage. Usually her father and another man will attend to this. Because of the heat shorter dresses are popular for bridesmaids, although the bride may still like to wear a traditional long dress.

Do not assume that you will be sitting at the top table alongside the bride and groom. If it is a small wedding reception with a large family contingent from the immediate family the room would look unbalanced if there were a huge top table with only three tables of guests. So the catering or banqueting manager may suggest to the hosts that the bridesmaids are placed on a young people's table.

With one Australian in four being an immigrant or second generation immigrant large numbers of ethnic weddings are held with relatives arriving from the Far East and Europe.

WEDDING SHOWS AND EVENTS

Wedding shows are held at major hotels in the large cities, and it is very helpful to visit such a show with the bride.

The bride and bridesmaids might like to have a pre-wedding hen party (shower tea in Australian). Only one shower tea is arranged, unlike America where many shower parties are held. The men have a bucks' night. Flower girls are popular in Australia as they are in America.

SEVENTH DAY ADVENTIST WEDDINGS

Seventh Day Adventists are Christians who celebrate

their sabbath on Saturday so weddings are held on other days of the week. Modest and inexpensive clothing is the rule but off-the-shoulder dresses would probably not cause any concern.

Seventh Day Adventists are vegetarian and abstain from alcohol. They also do not drink caffeinated drinks such as coffee, tea and cola drinks. Seventh Day Adventists sometimes provide non-vegetarian food and alcoholic drinks as a courtesy for the non-Seventh Day Adventist guests who are accustomed to it. At a Seventh Day Adventist wedding there is no smoking and no dancing, only background music.

NEW ZEALAND

On the south island Christchurch is known as the most English city outside England, whilst Dunedin is very Scottish. Bagpipers and Scottish dancing groups are available to provide entertainment. A more offbeat wedding night might include bride and groom walking to the end of the jetty and going off in a boat. In the mountain ski areas towards Mount Cook the bride and groom might arrive at the reception by helicopter.

MAORI WEDDINGS

Maori Weddings are likely to take place in Rotarua, the Maori centre, where something like fifty per cent of the population is Maori. Many pupils now attend bilingual schools so an increasing number of marriage services will be held in the Maori language. Maoris are Christian so the wedding might be held in church.

Weddings also take place in the communal meeting house. You would need to read about this in advance as the protocol is quite detailed. Individuals are greeted with a Maori hand clasp and the pressing of noses together. The first occasion when you visit a meeting place you must join a group for an official welcoming ceremony which involves a welcoming speech by the elders and a response from a representative of the visitors.

OTHER COUNTRIES

ARGENTINA

Here is an amusing idea you might like to copy. In Argentina ribbons are hung from the wedding cake. The bridesmaids pull out the ribbons and she who finds a symbolic ring attached to her ribbon is supposed to be the next bride.

CARIBBEAN

West Indian weddings in the UK can have as many as ten bridesmaids. After formal speeches many wellwishers stand up at tables all over the room and represent themselves and those not attending 'speaking for myself and Aunt Mathilda in Trinidad'.

Caribbean weddings may be chosen for a get-away-from-it-all second marriage and by couples where either the bride or groom has family from the Caribbean. In the Caribbean the wedding can take place on a beach or a boat. Wear a ballerina-length dress (calf length) not a long dress on the sand. High-necked dresses would be hot, although weddings are timed for late afternoon when it is cooler.

ISRAEL

A long summer enables Israeli Jewish weddings to take place outdoors under a bridal canopy symbolizing the home. Ceremonies in a synagogue require formal dress, but you can be much less formal if outdoors, at a kibbutz or on the beach.

POLYNESIA

The bridegroom arrives in a canoe and the couple are carried by four warriors. Women wear flowers in their hair. In Tahiti and Fiji the bride and bridesmaids can be provided with a grass skirt or pareo. In Fiji traditional Fijian dress may be worn of Tata cloth made from tree bark imprinted with native designs.

INDEX

THE FAMILY MATTERS SERIES